Quality Essentials

A Reference Guide from A to Z

Also available from ASQ Quality Press:

The Quality Improvement Handbook
ASQ Quality Management Division
John E. Bauer, Grace L. Duffy, Russell T. Westcott, editors

Quality's Greatest Hits: Classic Wisdom from the Leaders of Quality
Zigmund Bluvband

The Quality Improvement Glossary
Don Siebels

Quality Quotes
Helio Gomes

The Quality Toolbox
Nancy R. Tague

Business Process Improvement Toolbox
Bjørn Andersen

Six Sigma Project Management: A Pocket Guide
Jeffrey N. Lowenthal

Defining and Analyzing a Business Process: A Six-Sigma Pocket Guide
Jeffrey N. Lowenthal

To request a complimentary catalog of ASQ Quality Press publications, call 800-248-1946, or visit our Web site at http://qualitypress.asq.org.

Quality Essentials

A Reference Guide from A to Z

Jack B. ReVelle, PhD

ASQ Quality Press
Milwaukee, Wisconsin

American Society for Quality, Quality Press, Milwaukee 53203
© 2004 by ASQ
All rights reserved. Published 2004
Printed in the United States of America

12 11 10 09 08 07 06 05 04   5 4 3 2 1

Library of Congress Cataloging-in-Publication Data

ReVelle, Jack B.
   Quality essentials : a reference guide from A to Z / Jack B. ReVelle.
      p. cm.
   Includes bibliographical references and index.
   ISBN 0-87389-618-1 (Soft cover, perfect bound : alk. paper)
   1. Quality control. I. Title.

TS156.R468 2004
658.5'62—dc22   2004001466

ISBN 0-87389-618-1

Publisher: William A. Tony
Acquisitions Editor: Annemieke Hytinen
Project Editor: Paul O'Mara
Production Administrator: Randall Benson
Special Marketing Representative: Matt Meinholz

ASQ Mission: The American Society for Quality advances individual,
organizational, and community excellence worldwide through learning,
quality improvement, and knowledge exchange.

Attention Bookstores, Wholesalers, Schools, and Corporations: ASQ Quality
Press books, videotapes, audiotapes, and software are available at quantity
discounts with bulk purchases for business, educational, or instructional use.
For information, please contact ASQ Quality Press at 800-248-1946, or write to
ASQ Quality Press, P.O. Box 3005, Milwaukee, WI 53201-3005.

To place orders or to request a free copy of the ASQ Quality Press Publications
Catalog, including ASQ membership information, call 800-248-1946. Visit our
Web site at www.asq.org or http://qualitypress.asq.org.

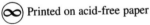 Printed on acid-free paper

Quality Press
600 N. Plankinton Avenue
Milwaukee, Wisconsin 53203
Call toll free 800-248-1946
Fax 414-272-1734
www.asq.org
http://qualitypress.asq.org
http://standardsgroup.asq.org
E-mail: authors@asq.org

To Bren, my wife and companion through more than 35 years of good times and bad, my greatest supporter and most severe critic. Whatever good I have achieved and whatever positive results I have attained, I owe to your valuable guidance. You have my love and appreciation always.

To Karen, our daughter, we love you and respect you, both for your funny, personal style and your serious, professional progress. From your earliest artistic success more than 25 years ago to the clever cover you designed for this book, we have watched you mature into the fine woman you are today.

To you both, many thanks for tolerating my idiosyncrasies, supporting my goals, and your love.

Table of Contents

List of Figures and Tables

Foreword

I first met Jack ReVelle in 1969 when we were both PhD candidates in industrial engineering and management at Oklahoma State University. As I recall, we never discussed our personal goals, but it was clear to me, as well as to others, that Jack was driven to lead in the overlapping areas of quality assurance and continuous improvement.

Since that time, our paths have crossed a number of times as officers of the Institute of Industrial Engineers, as members of the American Society for Quality Research Collaborative, and as instructors for National Technological University.

During this period, Jack has authored, coauthored, edited, coedited, or contributed chapters to more than 20 books and handbooks about quality assurance, continuous improvement, best practices, and safety. This is in addition to writing numerous articles, several of which won national awards.

When Jack called me with his request that I provide a foreword to this book, I asked him to send me a preview copy to review so that I could make an informed decision. He did, and I read it with the obvious result that I decided to write this foreword.

When you use this book as Jack intends it to be used, as a quality reference guide, you'll realize why I agreed to write this foreword. As a direct result of the selection of topics, the reader-friendly writing, the clever cartoons, as well as the excellent tables and figures, this is a *must have* reference guide to the most current approach to quality assurance (QA), continuous improvement (kaizen), total quality management (TQM), and Six Sigma. What's more, my bet is that you'll find this book to be indispensable, whether you are a quality newcomer or a seasoned pro.

I am proud that ASQ Quality Press decided to publish this book, and I urge members of ASQ to make it their next professional purchase and add it to their collection of quality reference books.

Kenneth E. Case, PhD, PE
Regents Professor
Industrial Engineering and Management
Oklahoma State University
Past President, Institute of Industrial Engineers
President, ASQ

Preface

I've been a researcher, a trainer, a university professor, a practitioner, a consultant, a speaker, and an author on Six Sigma, total quality, and continuous improvement for more than 30 years. I am currently an independent consultant who provides advice and assistance on these topics to senior executives in business and industry. Prior to this, I was the director of the center for process improvement for GenCorp Aerojet in Azusa and Sacramento, California, an aerospace and defense firm. I was responsible for leading its continuing quest for operational excellence. This was accomplished through the application of key initiatives such as Six Sigma, Malcolm Baldrige National Quality Award criteria, high-performance workplace, and supply chain management.

Previously, as the leader of continuous improvement for Hughes (now Raytheon) Missile Systems Company in Tucson, Arizona, I led a cross-functional team of employees for four years as we prepared and submitted our winning applications for the Arizona Pioneer Award for Quality in 1994 and the Arizona Governor's Award for Quality in 1997.

Throughout this broad variety of roles I have undertaken, I've consistently found a persistent and disturbing thread. It seems that no matter with whom I'm speaking, there are virtually always some misunderstandings or missing aspects of the facts. I suspect this occurs from a combination of factors, some over which we have no control. (Dr. Genichi Taguchi would refer to these as *noise* factors). But this book isn't about why the situation exists; it's about overcoming this situation with the facts.

Several years ago, when I first began to write brief snippets of this book, it was intended to be much smaller. However, the more people who reviewed the manuscript, the more suggestions I received regarding the inclusion of additional topics. But just as a manufacturer of cars must stop designing once a year and produce its annual models, so I have to do the same. Where understanding of a particular topic could be enhanced through the presentation of some simple graphics, these have been included.

The format of the book is unusual, but not unique. It is patterned after a book by Robert Townsend, former chairman and CEO of Avis, entitled *Up the Organization*. In addition to being interested in what the author had to say, I found that its alphabetized list of topics permitted the option of reading the book from cover to cover in a traditional approach or, and this is what I found exciting, reading those portions of the book that interested me at any given point in time and returning to the book at another time to learn more about other topics that were then at the top of my list. This book is designed to give readers the same options.

My target audience for this book varies extensively: from industrial, manufacturing, and quality engineers, supervisors and managers at the operational level all the way to the executive levels of an organization. These are the folks who both need and desire better understanding of the philosophy and practice of Six Sigma, total quality, and continuous improvement. And by the way, these folks aren't found just in big companies in the manufacturing sector. They are also found throughout small- and medium-sized businesses, service organizations, healthcare centers, homebuilders, educational institutions, and at all levels of government.

That's my story. I believe it's the best writing effort I've produced so far and I'm looking forward to seeing it reach the hands and minds of those who really have need for its contents.

Jack B. ReVelle, PhD
A Consulting Statistician
The Wizard of Odds
ReVelle Solutions
Tustin, California

Acknowledgments

It should come as no surprise that several people deserve special recognition for their exceptional contributions to the preparation of this book. To Karen ReVelle, my sincere appreciation for the excellent layout, color selection, and artwork for the covers of both the original and current editions. To Dean Elston, who created all the fine cartoons sprinkled throughout the book, many thanks for adding a much needed sense of fun. To Linda Gonet, a Six Sigma Green Belt, who created the graphics and then typed and organized the original manuscript, your help is always a confidence builder. And to Maria Muto, who finalized the manuscript for this edition with her consistent professional touch, I truly value your expert assistance.

Introduction

All work can be defined as a *process*, whether your point of reference is business services, commercial or industrial products, nonprofit products or services, educational services, healthcare services, government products or services, residential construction, or volunteer operations. The concept of process is described on page 135.

At the beginning of the total quality movement, it was not uncommon to hear the phrase, "Do it right the first time." As time passed, it became more and more obvious that doing it right the first time just wasn't enough to ensure continuous customer satisfaction. Thus, you are now more likely to hear the more accurate expansion: "Do the right things right the first time."

In Figure 1, the cook and the server appear to have agreed that one of them should be responsible to burn the toast while the other should scrape it. If we ignore the importance of continuous improvement, then their approach to the division of labor is reasonable. First, they're going to add an additional step or task to the existing process to attempt to overcome, but not eliminate, the problem. Of course, this means an increased cycle time and additional cost to produce the product with no guarantee that the fix will do the trick.

It seems this well-intentioned pair have overlooked the necessity of using data to determine the source(s) of the burnt toast and, subsequently, to eliminate the problem. The combined use of a few of the tools presented in this book would quickly lead them to understand and eliminate the source or sources of the root cause(s). Both the cook and the server demonstrate their individual and combined concerns regarding how to best satisfy their customers' tastes.

Figure 1 Do the right things right the first time.

There is a related concept referred to as the *voice of the customer*. It is important to understand, however, that there is more than just a single voice. In fact, there are many closely related voices, all demanding an attentive and ongoing audience. This brings us to the next figure. I created the underlying concept about 15 years ago and call it *the quality concert*.

In Figure 2, the *quality quartet* is composed of four voices: the customer, the engineer, the process (using the language of data), and management. Each member of the quality quartet offers a different, but important, aspect to the overall harmony of the quality concert. Each one provides a unique perspective on quality, total quality, Six Sigma, and continuous improvement.

The *quality chorus*, a multitude of voices, blends to support the quality concert. Just as in the world of music, where you hear sopranos, altos, baritones, and the like, the quality chorus has three primary voices: the society in which we live, the environment that supports our lives, and the governments that (are supposed to) do our bidding. Each voice emanates from its own vantage point as it relates to quality, total quality, Six Sigma, and continuous improvement.

Figure 2   The quality concert.

Located between the quality quartet and the quality chorus is a piano player with an instrument. This pairing of a person with a device suggests that sometimes a facilitator or coordinator is needed to complete unfinished ideas that bring the quartet and the chorus into a state of virtual harmony. Together, the quality quartet, the quality chorus, and the facilitator compose the quality concert. Every voice helps suppliers produce better and better products and services that are increasingly responsive to all the voices.

This leads us to the final introductory topic, which focuses on data: current, pertinent, valid, and sufficient data. Without this data, you're just another person with an opinion.

Figure 3 shows how in the absence of measurements, you have myth. No doubt about it: if you're not measuring, you're just practicing. There is a superabundance of total quality management (TQM), Six Sigma (6σ), and continuous improvement (CI) tools found in this book to assist you and your teammates in selecting, collecting, and analyzing data as well as selecting and solving the right problems quickly.

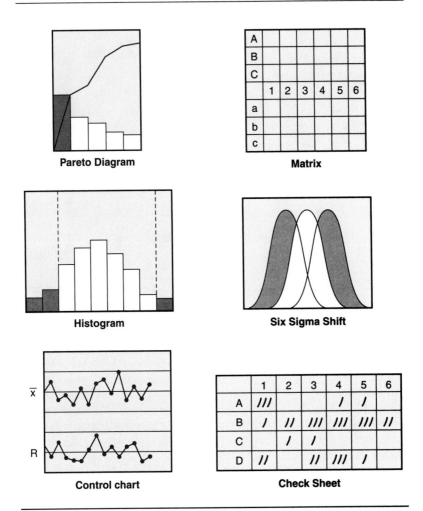

Figure 3 In the absence of measurements you have myth.

ACTIVITY BASED COSTING (ABC)

Activity based costing (ABC) is a management accounting system that assigns costs to products based on the amount of resources used to design, obtain, or make a product. These resources include floor space, raw materials, machine hours, inspection and test devices, utilities, and human effort.

ABC was developed so that management could determine the actual unit cost of production. Before its advent, management used standard costing, a system that allocates costs to products based on the number of machine and labor hours made available to a production department for a specific time period. Unfortunately, standard cost systems encourage managers to produce either unneeded products or the wrong mix of products so their department's cost per unit is minimized. Minimal cost per unit is achieved by fully utilizing both machines and labor.

ABC provides data-based insights to management, that otherwise would not be available, to facilitate important decisions relative to machine and labor assignments.

ACTIVITY NETWORK DIAGRAM (AND)

Developed in Japan during the 1980s, the activity network diagram (AND) is a derivative of the critical path method (CPM) and the program evaluation and review technique (PERT) that originated in

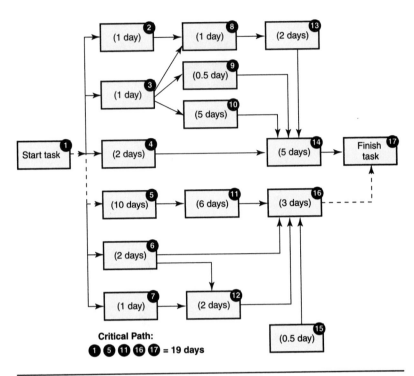

Figure 4   Activity network diagram.

the United States in the 1950s. CPM resulted from a joint project by DuPont and Remington Rand Univac in 1957. The goal of this project was to determine how to best reduce the time to perform routine plant overhaul, maintenance, and construction work. PERT was first used by the U.S. Navy in the design and production of the Polaris ICBM.

The AND is a tool for determining the optimal time for accomplishing a task and for graphically displaying the flow of activities that lead to its achievement (see Figure 4).

An AND is most effective when the activities for a task are well known and there is a high degree of confidence in that knowledge. Each activity is plotted in sequence, the time to accomplish each activity is annotated on the plot, and then the times are used to determine the earliest and latest possible times that any given activity can begin.

An AND clearly indicates which activities can be performed in parallel (concurrently) and which must be accomplished in sequence.

In this way, the optimal activity flow can be determined, and the minimum time to complete the entire task can be calculated.

If the activities are not well known and understood, a high level of frustration can result. When this is the case, the process decision program chart (PDPC) is a better tool for graphically displaying the flow of activities leading to a task or a project.

AFFINITY ANALYSIS

Affinity analysis, using affinity diagrams, is one of the seven management and planning tools. This popular tool is used when there is a need to identify major themes from a large number of ideas, opinions, or issues. It provides an easy-to-understand, easy-to-use approach in grouping those items that are naturally related, and then identifies the one concept generic enough that it ties each grouping together (see Figure 5).

The planning process begins with the collection of a large set of qualitative data regarding ideas, opinions, perceptions, desires, and

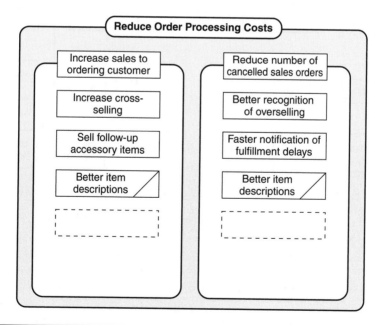

Figure 5   Refine groupings.

issues. Initially, the relationships among these data will not be clear, although there may be a sense of direction by the team.

Affinity analysis is a creative process, as opposed to being a logical process; it helps generate consensus by sorting written documents in lieu of discussing ideas (see Figure 6). These documents can be note cards or self-sticking note papers. The latter are preferred for use on walls, whiteboards, or windows.

Affinity analysis is the appropriate tool to use in the following circumstances: when chaos exists, when a team is overwhelmed by a surplus of ideas, when breakthrough thinking is needed, or when broad issues or themes must be identified.

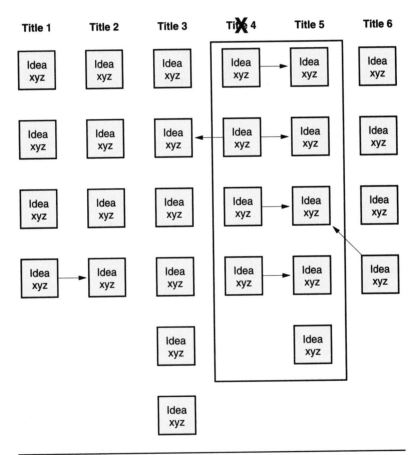

Figure 6   Further refinement.

AGILE ENTERPRISE

An agile enterprise (or agile organization) aggressively embraces change. To be agile is to be capable of operating profitably in a highly competitive environment of continually, and unpredictably, changing customer opportunities. Agility has emerged as the successor to mass production.

Agility is a comprehensive response to the business challenges of profiting from rapidly changing and continually fragmenting global markets for high-quality, high-performance, customer-configured goods and services. It is a continual readiness to change, sometimes radically, what companies and people must do and how they will do it.

The transition to agility is justified by the vision of sharing in highly profitable markets for information- and service-rich products configured to the requirements of individual customers.

An agile enterprise is one whose organizational structures and administrative processes enable fast and fluid translations of this initiative into customer-enriching business activities.

AGILE ENTERPRISE VERSUS LEAN ENTERPRISE

An agile enterprise goes well beyond the marketing strategy known as lean enterprise in that it permits the customer, jointly with the supplier, to determine the nature of the product.

In a lean enterprise organization, a customer burden exists. The challenge is that the broad range of customer choices is driven by producers who declare that customers will have a broad range of choices; however, these choices are selected by the producers. Within an agile enterprise, choice is driven by the consumers.

Both the organization and the methods of lean enterprise are key components for an organization becoming an agile enterprise. Enterprises should pass through *lean* before *agile* (see Figure 7). Skipping *lean* is both expensive and wasteful.

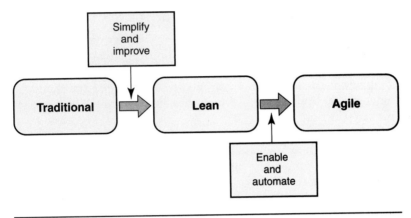

Figure 7   Enterprise transformation process.

ANALYTIC HIERARCHY PROCESS (AHP)

The analytic hierarchy process (AHP) was formalized and popularized by Tom Saaty.* AHP is used to help develop weights, values, and priorities for concepts, products, options, and other items of importance. This multicriteria decision-support process employs a one-to-nine scale when making paired comparisons:

1 = *equal importance:* the row and column have the same impact upon the higher order need.

3 = *moderate importance:* experience and judgment slightly favor the row over the column.

5 = *strong importance:* experience and judgment strongly favor the row over the column.

7 = *very strong importance:* the row is strongly favored and its dominance is demonstrated in practice.

9 = *extreme importance:* the evidence favoring the row is of the highest possible order of affirmation.

This nine-point scale is worded for the situation when the row in a paired comparison matrix is more important than the column.

---

* Thomas L. Saaty, *Fundamentals of Decision Making and Priority Theory with the Analytic Hierarchy Process* (Pittsburgh: RWS Publications, 1994). Chap. 1, "How to Make a Decision," provides a good summary of AHP.

Table 1   AHP matrix example.

	A	B	C
A	1	1/5	1/3
B	5	1	9
C	3	1/9	1

For example, when the topic in the row and column are the same, a point value of one is selected. This occurs on the diagonal from the top left to the bottom right.

When the row topic (*B*) is determined to be extremely important when compared to the column topic (*C*), a value of nine is entered in the matrix, as shown in Table 1.

A full, pairwise comparison yields ratio data. A ratio scale includes an absolute zero. With an absolute zero, finding ratios and multiplying numbers has meaning. It is tempting to treat any number as ratio data, even when it is not appropriate. To avoid this error, AHP should be used to create ratio data for ranking.

BAR CHART

A bar chart is a form of graphic presentation designed to quickly and simply communicate quantitative information. It always has two dimensions: the horizontal axis, or x-axis, that is traditionally used for an independent variable, and the vertical axis, or y-axis, that is used to describe the dependent variable.

The independent variable can be either variable/continuous data or attribute/discrete data. A histogram is a bar chart that presents variable/continuous data as the independent variable. A Pareto diagram is a bar chart using attribute/discrete data as the independent variable. Both histograms and Pareto diagrams use the vertical axis to communicate about *frequency of occurrence.*

A bar chart can be displayed with the bars oriented either vertically or horizontally, depending on the inclination and needs of the chartmaster.

BENCHMARKING: TECHNICAL VERSUS COMPETITIVE

Benchmarking is the process of measuring products, services, and processes against those organizations known to be leaders in one or more aspects of their operations. Benchmarking can be of great help to an organization by providing necessary insights to understand how one organization compares with similar organizations, even if those other organizations are in a different business or have a different group of customers. Additionally, benchmarking can help an organization identify areas, systems, or processes for improvements— either incremental (continuous) improvements or dramatic (business process reengineering) improvements. Benchmarking has been classified into two distinct categories: competitive benchmarking and technical benchmarking.

Competitive benchmarking is necessary to compare how well (or poorly) an organization is doing with respect to the leading competition, especially with respect to critically important attributes, functions, or values associated with the organization's products or services. For example, on a scale of one to five, five being best, how do customers rank the organization's products or services compared to those of the leading competition? If hard data cannot be provided, marketing efforts may be misdirected and design efforts misguided.

Technical benchmarking is performed by the design staff to ascertain the capabilities of products or services, especially in comparison to the products or services of leading competitors. For example, on a scale of one to four, four being best, how do designers rank the properties of the organization's products or services? If hard data cannot be supplied, the design efforts may be insufficient and products or services inadequate to be competitive.

Technical Benchmarking

Technical benchmarking means determining how well both an organization and the competition are fulfilling customer needs in terms of design requirements. This evaluation is expressed as a score plotted on the vertical axis. Some score the design requirements on a scale of one to four, with four being the best. This method results in a plot across the bottom of the house of quality (quality function deployment). Figure 8 illustrates how these features are entered.

Competitive Benchmarking

Another addition (room) is added on the right side of the house of quality to reflect how well an organization and the competition are satisfying the customer requirements (identified on the vertical axis on the left side of the matrix). As in the case of technical benchmarking, this evaluation is plotted as a graph.

Comparing the results of the technical and competitive benchmarking data should show a consistency. If a product scores high in

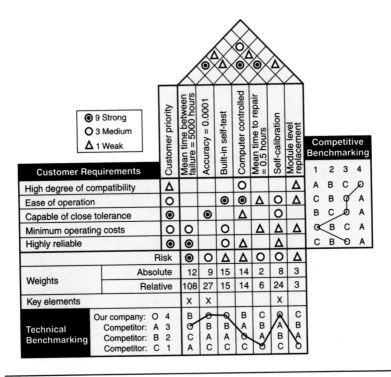

Figure 8   Benchmarking: house of quality.

the competitive comparison, it should also score high on the technical comparison. Inconsistencies are flags that there may be a problem with a design requirement.

More columns can be added to the right side of the matrix to
include other information, as needed. The possibilities are unlim-
ited and should be driven by a team's imagination and capacity for
innovation.

This completes the house of quality. This information is given to
each of the appropriate organizations and ad hoc teams developing
the products and services. The integrated product and process
development (IPPD) team then manages the development of the
other matrices to ensure the complete and effective design and
development of the customer offering.

Target Values

It is necessary to establish target values for each design requirement.
This action establishes concrete goals for the design engineers and
further defines customer requirements. These values need to be

measurable and can be developed from historical records, designed experiments, or analysis of what the competition is doing. Once the team agrees on the target values, they are entered on the horizontal axis with the design requirements.

BOX AND WHISKER CHART

A box and whisker chart (boxplot) is used to simultaneously display the median (measure of central tendency) and the two center quartiles (measure of dispersion). This presents a more complete picture of the status of a process.

Figure 9 shows what can be done with a data set that may not be normally distributed other than using the mean and standard deviation to create a frequency distribution.

In a box and whisker chart, the top of the box is the data point at the top of the second quartile, and the bottom of the box is the data point at the bottom of the third quartile. In Figure 10's data pool, the top of the box would correspond to a value of 44, the center of the box would correspond to the median (39), and the bottom

Data Pool (n = 20)	Quartile			
	1st	**2nd**	**3rd**	**4th**
	50	44	38	34
	49	43	38	33
	47	42	37	32
	45	41	36	31
	45	40	35	30
		Median = 39		

Figure 9 A data set not normally distributed.

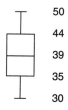

Figure 10 Box and whisker chart.

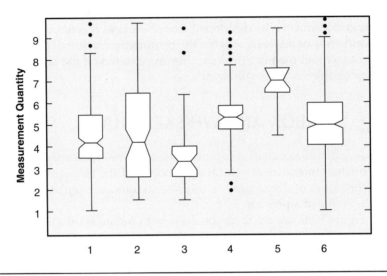

Figure 11 More complex box plots.

of the box would have a value of 35. The far end of the top whisker would be 50 and the far end of the bottom whisker would be 30. Figure 11 shows a more complex box plot presentation.

BRAINSTORMING: CLASSICAL VERSUS 635 VERSUS IMAGINARY

Classical Brainstorming

The cornerstone or foundation of judgmentally based decisions is the generation of creative alternatives. The purpose of classical brainstorming is to place as many ideas as possible out on a table, where they can be discussed and evaluated, and to draw upon all the knowledge and experience of team members.

Classical brainstorming is a technique used to generate multiple ideas by a team. Similar to the nominal group technique, it is useful in identifying problems, determining their causes, and generating their solutions. Properly conducted, a classical brainstorming session will produce a maximum quantity of potential ideas in a minimum amount of time by fully utilizing the collective creativity of a team.

Classical brainstorming has been used successfully to identify problems, establish organizational goals and objectives, construct process flowcharts and process maps, expedite cause-and-effect analysis, and search out potential corrective actions.

The basic ground rules of classical brainstorming are quite straightforward:

- No criticism
- Get crazy
- Quantity, not quality
- Group effort

Figure 12 describes interrelationships between these ground rules.

Brainstorming 635

Brainstorming 635 was named after the way it is conducted. Usually six people write three ideas and pass the ideas around their circle about every five minutes. During the process of idea generation, the participants take ideas produced by other team members and attempt to develop them further.

Brainstorming 635 can be used when a team needs another technique for producing additional ideas. It is a viable alternative to classical brainstorming when personalities or team dynamics require a different approach because team members come from different levels of an organization. It is also effective when a problem requires additional analytical thinking. Brainstorming 635 is especially recommended when the number of participants makes classical brainstorming impractical. With many people, several 635 groups can be established, or the worksheets can be passed fewer times.

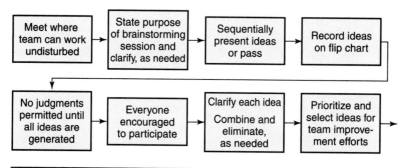

Figure 12　Interrelationships between ground rules of classical brainstorming.

Brainstorming 635 is accomplished without discussion or conversation of any kind. Team members write down three ideas and pass their papers to the person on their right (only for the sake of tradition). They read these silently and add three more ideas that are triggered by the preceding ideas. This continues around the circle until each person gets back his or her original paper. Brainstorming 635 uses a silent, iterative approach, and it encourages more reflection than does classical brainstorming. With this approach, the potential exists for 108 ideas to be generated in 30 minutes.

Imaginary Brainstorming

The unique approach used by imaginary brainstorming encourages the generation of unusual ideas. To begin, classical brainstorming is conducted, and then a single item in the original brainstorming description is altered. This is followed by the generation of new ideas based on the altered description. The results of the imaginary brainstorming are then compared to the original results. This is portrayed in Figure 13.

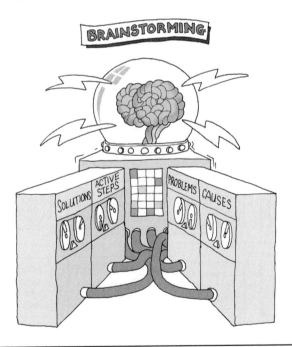

Figure 13   Comparing the results of imaginary brainstorming to the original results.

Imaginary brainstorming helps break established patterns of thinking, allowing a team to identify more creative ideas and solutions to problems.

BUSINESS PROCESS REENGINEERING (BPR)

Business process reengineering (BPR) is the use of information technology to radically redesign business processes to achieve dramatic improvements in their performance. In this context, reengineering is the fundamental rethinking of everything associated with organizational processes.

BPR is not the introduction of automation, rewriting of software, or organizational restructuring, downsizing, or rightsizing.

BPR is a new beginning, that is, starting over with a clean piece of paper, rejecting conventional wisdom, and inventing new approaches to process structure. The admonition to *think outside of the box* clearly conveys the intent of business process reengineering.

The organizational determination that the introduction of continuous improvement (CI) would not provide sufficient nor desired results and that BPR is required to achieve these results necessitates the formal application of a filtering process to ascertain whether or not the specific problem or area of concern meets or exceeds the criteria to justify selection of BPR. (See *CI versus BPR,* page 22.)

CAUSE-AND-EFFECT ANALYSIS

The original concept of brainstorming as a means to generate and collect possible causes of a specific effect (either positive or negative) offers minimal structure to assist members of a cross-functional team. Cause-and-effect analysis was developed in the 1950s by Dr. Kaoru Ishikawa to provide the structure missing from traditional brainstorming.

Cause-and-effect analysis is sometimes referred to as the Ishikawa diagram, but perhaps more frequently as the fishbone diagram because of its similarity in appearance to the skeleton of a fish (see Figure 14).

As a team generates possible causes or ideas using brainstorming, these ideas are placed on the diagram by the team leader or facilitator. This contributes to more efficient analysis and evaluation of the causes by graphically establishing the relationships between and among these various ideas. The *effect* is generally described as a *problem* to facilitate brainstorming of the potential causes.

Cause-and-effect analysis helps team members identify which factors (independent variables) could, either directly or indirectly, contribute to the effect (dependent variable) being studied. Usually one or more of these *five Ms and an E* are the primary sources or causes of the effect:

- Men/women
- Machine
- Measurement
- Material
- Method
- Environment

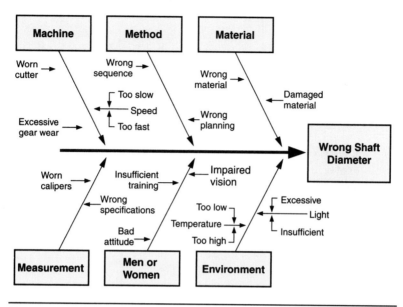

Figure 14 Ishikawa or fishbone diagram.

CHART/GRAPH

A chart or graph, in the context of continuous improvement (CI), is a diagram or figure that provides a pictorial illustration of data.

A chart or graph contains data that represent the inherent variation of an entity, especially in comparison with that of one or more other entities. First, data are collected, then organized as a table according to some criteria, and finally presented as a chart or graph. It is in this final step that data become information used to facilitate enlightened decision making. Ultimately, data can become knowledge containing insights and understanding that, in its raw state, might not otherwise be available.

There are many types of charts and graphs. For example, within the seven quality control tools, there are the Pareto diagram, the histogram, the scatter diagram, and any one of the several control charts: x-bar and R, c, p, np, and u. Within the seven management planning tools, there are the affinity diagram, the interrelationship digraph, the tree diagram, and the matrix diagram. Some conventional examples of charts and graphs are shown in Figure 15.

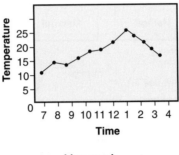

Line graph

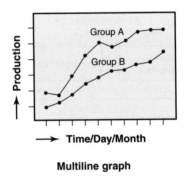

Multiline graph

Circle graph

Figure 15 Conventional examples of charts and graphs. *continued*

continued

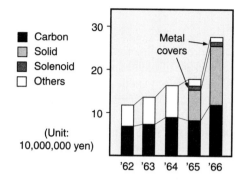

Compound bar graph

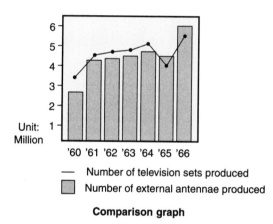

— Number of television sets produced

▨ Number of external antennae produced

Comparison graph

Multicomponent bar graph

Figure 15　Conventional examples of charts and graphs.

CHECK SHEETS AND CHECKLISTS

Check sheets or checklists provide a systematic method for collecting and displaying specific data. In most cases, check sheets are forms designed for the purpose of collecting specific data. They provide a consistent, effective, and economical approach to gathering data, organizing it for analysis, and displaying it for preliminary review (see Figure 16).

Check sheets sometimes take the form of manual check sheets where automated data are not necessary or available. Data figures and check sheets should be designed to minimize the need for complicated entries that encourage personnel error (see Figure 17). Properly designed, check sheets can facilitate development data summaries for other TQM or CI tools such as Pareto analysis and histograms.

Simple, straightforward tables are a key to successful data gathering.

Defect	Supplier				Total
	A	B	C	D	
Incorrect invoice	////	/		//	7
Incorrect inventory	̵ℋ̵ℋ̵	//	/	/	9
Damaged material	///		//	///	8
Incorrect test document	/	///	////	//	10
Total	13	6	7	8	34

Figure 16   Checklist to collect supplier data.

	Deviation	Checks				5					10					15					20	Frequency
	10																					
	9																					
Upper spec	8																					
	7																					
	6	X																				1
	5	X																				1
	4	X	X																			2
	3	X	X	X																		3
	2	X	X	X	X	X	X	X														7
	1	X	X	X	X	X	X	X	X													8
Target spec	0	X	X	X	X	X	X	X	X	X	X	X										11
	–1	X	X	X	X	X	X	X	X	X												9
	–2	X	X	X	X	X	X															6
	–3	X	X	X	X																	4
	–4	X	X																			2
	–5	X																				1
	–6																					
	–7																					
Lower spec	–8																					
	–9																					
	–10																					
																					Total	55

Figure 17 Check sheet for data distribution.

CONCURRENT ENGINEERING/SIMULTANEOUS ENGINEERING (CE/SE)

Concurrent engineering (originally known as simultaneous engineering) refers to a systematic approach developed to ensure the integrated, parallel design of products and their related processes. Of necessity, this approach includes personnel selected carefully from engineering, tooling, and manufacturing as well as from test and support activities.

The goals of concurrent engineering (CE) are to optimize and coordinate all critical product and process characteristics. The employment of the CE design process is known as integrated product and process development (IPPD). It begins with the establishment of cross-functional, multidisciplinary teams called integrated product and process development teams or IPTs.

IPTs are expected to address some very specific, parallel design activities in support of the goals. Each of these activities addresses a set of vital design requirements. In turn, each set of requirements impacts the others. It is this interrelationship that is missed or overlooked in the traditional serial or sequential design process. Concurrent engineering ensures that a final design provides for every aspect of each set of requirements. This results in a design that satisfies customer requirements, optimizes manufacturability, and satisfies regulatory requirements.

CONTINUOUS IMPROVEMENT VERSUS BUSINESS PROCESS REENGINEERING (CI VERSUS BPR)

It has been said that continuous improvement (CI) is like lighting a thousand candles under a steel plate and gradually warming it up, while business process reengineering (BPR) is like using a blowtorch to burn a hole through the plate.

Both the candles and the blowtorch use the same technique, combustion, and produce similar results, that is, the metal gets hotter.

The objective of the blowtorch, however, is to fundamentally alter the shape of the plate in a short period of time. BPR, likewise, attempts to produce a dramatic change in a portion of an organization over a relatively short period of time.

Continuous improvement programs, on the other hand, aim to produce incremental improvement throughout the organization over a much longer period of time.

Neither CI nor BPR is an organizational panacea: no single approach has the capability or intention of solving every organizational problem. One thing is clear, however: the first step towards achieving an optimal solution is the selection and application of the appropriate approach.

If it has been determined by the organization that the introduction of CI would not provide sufficient or desired results and that BPR is required to achieve these results, then it becomes necessary to formally apply a filtering process to ascertain whether or not the specific problem or area of concern meets or exceeds the criteria to justify selection of BPR.

CONTINUOUS IMPROVEMENT (CI): KAIZEN

A continuous improvement (CI) process is a disciplined methodology for understanding, analyzing, and continually improving business processes, capabilities, and procedures with the objective of meeting or exceeding customer desires.

Every organizational process has undiscovered opportunities for improvement waiting to be discovered. The use of structured methods that employ graphic techniques for analysis, measurement, and decision support leads to better solutions for continuous improvement.

Consistently meeting or exceeding customer expectations can best be achieved by having enabled and empowered people work together to improve organizational processes. The continuous improvement of an organization's processes, products, and services inevitably leads to fewer defects, reduced variation, lower costs, shorter cycle times, and improved productivity.

Continuous improvement comes from the Japanese concept of *kaizen.* In its fullest context, this term applies CI to one's personal life, home life, social life, and work life. At work, this translates to CI involving everyone in all aspects of the workplace. The most direct route to CI is the variability reduction process (VRP) (see Figure 18).

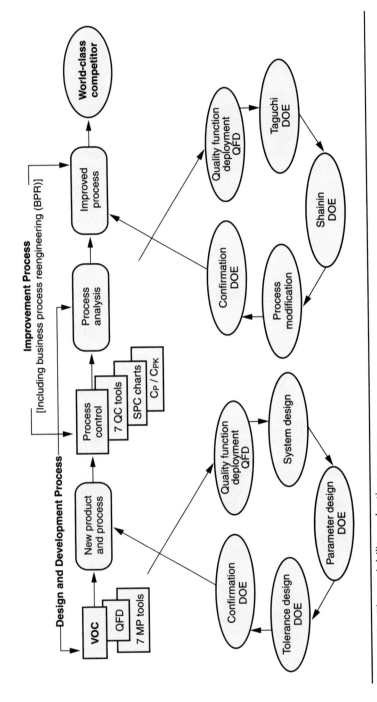

Figure 18   The variability reduction process.

CONTROL CHARTS

When processes require close surveillance of specific attributes as well as critical dimensions or rates during production, this status assessment is best accomplished with the application of control charts. The primary purpose of control charts is to graphically show trends in the frequency of occurrence of attributes or in the magnitude of dimensions or rates with respect to maximum and minimum limit lines (referred to as upper and lower control limits).

A process that has reached a state of statistical control has a predictable spread of quality and a predictable output. Control charts provide a means of anticipating and correcting any special causes (as opposed to common causes), that may be responsible for generating defects or unacceptable variation.

Control charts are used to direct the efforts of engineers (design, process, quality, manufacturing, industrial, and so on), operators, supervisors, and other process improvement team (PIT) members toward special causes when, and only when, a control chart detects the presence and influence of a special cause. The ultimate power of control charts lies in their ability to identify special (assignable) causes of defects and variation.

The objective of control chart analysis is to obtain evidence that the inherent process variability (the range or R) and the process average (the average of the averages or x-double bar) are no longer operating at stable (predictable) levels. When this occurs, one or both are out of control (unstable), so appropriate and timely corrective action should be introduced.

The purpose of establishing control charts is to distinguish between the inherent random variability of a process (common causes) and the variability attributed to an assignable (special) cause. Common causes are those that cannot be readily changed without significant process reengineering.

Control charts are used to study specific ongoing processes to keep them operating with minimal defects and variation. This operating state is known as Six Sigma and can be verified using performance measures such as C_P, the process capability index, and C_{PK}, the mean-sensitive process capability index. This is in contrast to downstream inspection and testing that aim to detect defects and variation after they have been generated by the process. In other words, control charts are focused on prevention rather than detection and rejection.

It has been confirmed in practice that economy and efficiency are better served by prevention than by detection. It costs as much to make a bad part as a good part, and the cost of control charts is repaid many times over as a direct result of improving production quality.

Types of Control Charts

Just as there are two types of data, variable/continuous and attribute/discrete, there are also two types of control charts: variables charts for use with continuous data and attributes charts for use with discrete data.

Variables control charts should be used whenever measurements from a product or process are available. The following are examples of continuous data: diameters, torque values, durations, temperatures, and electrical performance values such as voltages and amperages. Whenever possible, variables control charts are preferred to attributes control charts because they provide greater insights regarding product or process status.

When continuous data are not available, but discrete data are, then it is appropriate to use attributes control charts. There are only two levels for attribute data—conform/nonconform, pass/fail, go/no-go, present/absent; however, they can be counted, recorded, and analyzed. Examples of discrete data include: presence or position of a label, installation of all required fasteners, presence of excess or insufficient solder, and measurements recorded as accept/reject.

Figure 19 summarizes the various types of variables and attributes control charts, and Figure 20 indicates when they should be applied.

Characteristic Value	Name
Variable (Continuous)	$\bar{x}$–R chart (average value and range) x-MR chart (measured value and moving range)
Attribute (Discrete)	np chart (number of defective units) p chart (fraction defective) c chart (number of defects) u chart (number of defects per unit)

Figure 19 Types of control charts.

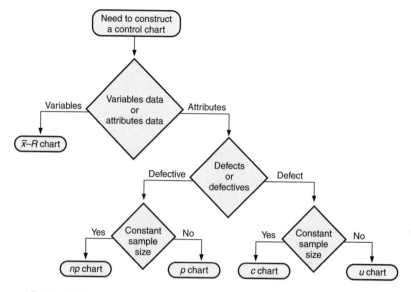

Defect = A failure to meet one part of an acceptance criteria.
Defective = A unit that fails to meet acceptance criteria due to one or more defects.

Figure 20   Determining which control chart to use.

COST OF QUALITY (COQ)

The cost of quality (COQ) has for many years been a tool primarily used within the quality world, that is, within the province of quality professionals. It is the total cost associated with making, finding, repairing, or preventing defects. The following categories are associated with these costs: internal failure costs, external failure costs, appraisal costs, and prevention costs.

Internal failure costs include all the costs associated with the following: scrap, rework, retest, downtime, yield losses, and disposition of nonconforming material.

External failure costs are those associated with defects detected after shipment to the customer: complaint adjustment, returned materials, warranty charges, and concessions due to nonconforming product.

Appraisal costs are those associated with evaluation of product condition or status during a product's first passage through the manufacturing and assembly process: incoming material inspection and test, in-process inspection and test, metrology, materials or services consumed in the appraisal process, yield losses, and disposition of nonconforming material.

Prevention costs are those incurred to keep failure and appraisal costs to a minimum: quality planning, new product review, training, process control, quality data acquisition and analysis, and quality reporting.

COQ is a common term used by quality professionals, but from company to company, it may be known by a variety of different names. One former client referred to it as the cost of poor execution (COPE).

Whatever a company chooses to call it, COQ is an important indicator of the effectiveness of a company's quality management system. It is important to relate the cost of quality to other operational data, for example, COQ as a percent of sales or compared to profit.

Another sound move is comparison of the various elements or categories of COQ with each other. For example, comparing the relationship of prevention costs with external failure costs. This data can be effective as indicators to assist in establishing priorities for improvement activities or evaluating operational effectiveness.

CRITICAL INCIDENTS TECHNIQUE

Between 1940 and 1960, extensive research was conducted on a developmental technique in which individuals were provided continual feedback on their critical behaviors. To begin, research was conducted to develop a list of positive and negative behaviors critical to the successful performance of a given job. For example, at the supervisory level, a negative critical behavior might be criticizing the work of a subordinate in the presence of other employees. A positive behavior might be effectively involving subordinates in problem solving or taking the initiative to solve a long-standing problem.

After an instrument is developed, the superior systematically develops a record as critical behaviors are observed. Continual feedback then provides a basis for behavior change. Although the critical incidents technique is not widely used, its results have been impressive, and the principles upon which it is based are sound. It takes place on the job and makes use of the organization's power structure. It provides regular feedback which, in turn, deals with behavior. It provides for positive reinforcement of desirable behaviors as well as discouraging undesirable ones.

Since the evaluation factor is built into the environment, a manager needs only to observe and make a record of behavior rather than to constantly make value judgments. The critical incidents technique should increasingly receive high marks as a developmental procedure.

CUSTOMER TABLE

The customer table is a simplification and explanation of the Kano model and is used in conjunction with quality function deployment (both discussed in this book). A customer table is employed to assist an organization in developing a complete and clear picture of what its customers expect to receive when they acquire its products or services. This applies for either external or internal customers.

External customers exist outside an organization and purchase its products and services. Internal customers are persons within an organization who receive the outputs of processes that exist upstream from their processes.

All customers are important. Failure to satisfy external customers will eventually cause the demise of an organization, while failure to satisfy internal customers will ultimately prevent an organization from satisfying its external customers.

These are summarized in Figure 21.

		Musts	Wants	Wows
Customer	External	Receive product ordered	Perceived value Easy to order Friendly service	Overnight delivery Free shipping
	Internal	Receive correct information	Easy-to-use processes To be treated like a customer	100% cooperation

Figure 21   A customer table—example.

CYCLE TIME MANAGEMENT (CTM)

Cycle time management (CTM) is a strategic management process used to significantly reduce cycle times in an organization. This dramatically increases an organization's productivity and profits. By focusing on cycle time as the performance measure of choice, organizations are able to reduce delivery times and to improve product and service quality, thus creating a more satisfied customer.

A company's total business cycle is measured from the time a customer's need is identified to receipt of payment from that customer for the finished product or service. Total business cycle time includes any or all of the following subcycles or loops:

- *Make/ship loop.* This is the time from receipt of material, through the value-adding material conversion steps, to shipment or transfer of a finished product to the distribution loop.

- *Distribution loop.* This is the time from finished production to shipment to the customer from the distribution warehouse.

- *Supply loop.* This is the time from release of the purchase order to receipt of the correct materials in the right quantities at the right point in the manufacturing process.

- *New product introduction loop.* This is the time from identification of the need for a new product or service to delivery of the first unit to a customer.

- *Strategic business development loop.* This is the time required to develop a new strategy, make the decision to adopt it, and then implement it.

In recent years, it has become increasingly evident that the compartmentalization of these loops has inhibited organizational competitiveness. All the loops must be integrated if the total business cycle is to be reduced.

Practice has proven that a time-driven approach to continuous improvement brings order to the selection of quality and productivity improvement projects. Instead of being overwhelmed by a large number of seemingly disjointed projects, an organization can integrate these projects at a higher level and implement changes in a systematic way. Time, then, becomes the overall measure of organizational performance.

Because CTM focuses on time, it helps organizations of all types to produce products and services of better quality at lower cost and with faster delivery.

Figure 22 is an example of CTM use.

The figure defines four stages:

1. *Vision.* This develops through CTM education that fosters executive awareness of the CTM concept and the opportunities it represents.

2. *Analysis.* A formal business assessment ensures that all the necessary prerequisites and requirements for a successful conversion to CTM are identified ahead of time and that most, if not all, have been provided.

3. *Implementation.* This stage encompasses a tightly controlled sequence of 12 steps divided into planning and execution phases. It outlines how education, planning, and execution can be integrated into full-scale development of the evolution plan. (Since CTM is such a radical departure from traditional operating practices, a total commitment to a sustained effort toward change is a prime prerequisite for successful implementation.)

4. *Competitive edge.* At the completion of the CTM implementation process, CTM will have become *a way of life.*

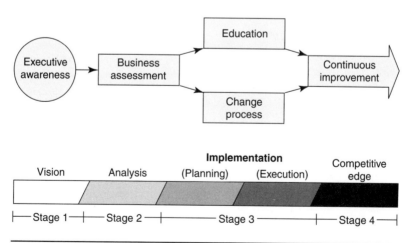

Figure 22   Road map to CTM implementation.

Cycle Time Management Guidelines

1. Evaluate "as is" (existing) process regarding need for change.

2. If *yes*, determine if kaizen methodology (continuous improvement) is sufficient.

3. If *yes*, implement kaizen. If *no*, then initiate use of process redesign/reengineering.

4. Differentiate between value-added, value enabling, and non-value-added steps in "as is" process.

5. Eliminate or reduce duration of non-value-added steps.

6. Identify and implement new and/or improved technologies to reduce duration of value enabling and value-added steps.

7. Locate and make use of opportunities to work steps in parallel rather than in series throughout the process.

8. Finalize the resulting new process.

9. Conduct pilot test to verify acceptability of resulting process.

10. Operationalize the new process.

DATA: ATTRIBUTE/DISCRETE VERSUS VARIABLE/CONTINUOUS

Attribute data, also known as discrete data, are counted in whole numbers or integers. An attribute is the presence or absence of a particular characteristic. The result will always be a whole number, that is, no fractions. Typically, whether something has a particular attribute can be answered as either *yes* or *no*. In working with products, services, and processes, items are classified as good versus bad, accept versus reject, go versus no-go, and the like. When dealing with such things as defects, or parts returned for rework or scrap, these are attribute data. Attribute data are much easier to collect and record than variable data but don't provide as much information about the subject items.

Variable data, also known as continuous data, are measurements from a continuous scale; these can be, and frequently are, decimal fractions. The accuracy of a measurement is a function of the level of sensitivity or precision of the measuring instrument being used. Clearly, more precise measurements can be obtained with more sensitive instrumentation. Variable data provide more information about product and process characteristics than attribute data but are more complex and time-consuming to collect and record.

DATA COLLECTION STRATEGY

"Without data, you're just another person with an opinion." "In God we trust, all others bring data." And so on. We collect data to help make better decisions than we would otherwise, both individually and collectively. Better decisions come from a reduction in uncertainty, instead of decisions based on guesswork, gut feel, or common sense. Data are facts, the performance measures, or metrics that someone has collected; however, they are not information ready to be used in making decisions.

For data to become ready for use by decision makers, they must lead to understanding. To correct a problem, we need to understand its nature and its causes. As data are collected and compared with desired performance levels, we are able to learn more about the causes or sources of a problem, what should be measured, and how it should be measured. This suggests a strategy for data collection.

The following is a partial checklist of steps that should be a part of the data collection strategy employed within an organization:

- Determine the purpose of the data to be collected. Will it be used to assess the status of a process or a product? Will it provide a basis for decisions regarding process or product quality?

- Determine the nature of the data to be collected. Is it measurable (variable or continuous) data or is it counted (attribute or discrete) data?

- Determine the characteristics of the data to be collected. Can the data be easily understood by persons who will evaluate product and process improvement (including customers)?

- Determine if the data can be expressed in terms that invite comparisons with similar processes. Can the performance metric/measure be expressed as *ppm* (parts per million), *dpmo* (defects per million defect opportunities), C_P or C_{PK} (process capability indices), or 6σ (Six Sigma)?

- Determine if the data place priority on the most important quality influences and if the data are economical and easy to collect.

- Determine the best type of data gathering check sheet to use: checklists, tally sheets, or defect density/concentration maps/diagrams.

- Determine if it will be possible to use some form of random sampling or whether it will be necessary to use 100 percent data collection.

DATA STRATIFICATION

The purpose of data stratification is to convert a heterogeneous population into a collection of homogeneous subpopulations. This separation process facilitates those studies or analyses of the heterogeneous population from which statistical samples may be drawn.

Examples of data stratification include analysis of a population of machines to determine which types create specific kinds of defects and/or excessive variation, examination of a population of defects created by a process to ascertain the *critical few* categories, and studies of a population of employees to identify the needs and expectations of each category of employees.

The procedure for data stratification is not complicated. Once the population of concern has been identified, it is examined to determine the various types of categories that exist therein: size (dimensions), age, vendor/supplier (sources), color, weight, distance, gender, and cost. Next, the population is stratified (divided) according to the pertinent categories. Then, finally, as data regarding the population are collected, the categorical information about the sampled units is recorded using a tally sheet or some other type of data table.

DEFECT MAP

When patterns of specific defects or excessive variation occur over time, it may be desirable to collect and log these patterns as a series of visual records. These records or defect maps are used to record the locations of the defects relative to the unit geometry.

Defect maps provide much-needed assistance in problem solving, that is, the focus moves to more detailed, lower-level problems that are easier to identify and correct. They are readily applied to both fabrication and assembly defects as well as to supplier problems.

The procedure is straightforward: create a clearly defined product sketch with identifying coordinates, collect and reduce the resulting data to usable statistics, and then focus subsequent problem solving on the critical few—the worst first. Figure 23 shows a template for a circuit card defect map.

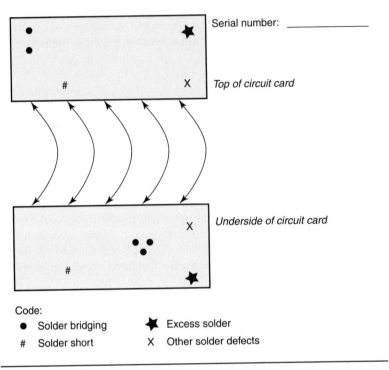

Code:
●   Solder bridging   ★ Excess solder
Solder short   X   Other solder defects

Figure 23   Defect map.

DELPHI METHOD

The day of the individual decision maker is virtually gone. Even at the highest levels of an organization, decisions are made by teams or groups of subject matter experts (SMEs) who come together to reach consensus on subjects of consequence.

The Delphi method provides a methodology to facilitate the merging of ideas, conclusions, beliefs, and in some cases, question-able facts. The application of this tool results in a rapid synthesis of data and/or information (not necessarily the same thing), whether the participants are in the same room or geographically dispersed.

The Delphi method is a nonquantitative technique that facilitates achievement of group consensus through a series of input–output iterations. The procedure begins with a team of persons, either exter-nal or internal to the organization; the team prepares a series of questions that are submitted to the participants.

Responses to each set of questions form the basis for the next set. Responses are circulated (in person, using snail mail, by e-mail, or via the Internet) so each participant can judge his or her alignment and rationale. If desired, members of the group may participate anonymously in the Delphi method.

DEMING CYCLE/SHEWHART CYCLE: PLAN–DO–CHECK/STUDY–ACT (PDCA/PDSA)

Dr. W. Edwards Deming, after whom Japan's Deming Prize for Quality is named, realized many years ago that innovation, improvements to systems, and reducing process and product variation require the use of a problem-solving process.

A key element in the development of such a process is the application of the plan–do–check/study–act cycle (PDCA/PDSA) (see Figure 24). This cycle is a repeatable sequence of activities for constant continuous improvement and innovation, enabling employees and suppliers to efficiently and effectively solve their problems as

Plan	Before taking action, plan what change or improvement is needed and how it will be achieved.	Identify area of opportunity. Form team and define process. Select project. Collect and analyze data. Data identifies problem?
Do	Implement planned change or improvement on a small scale.	Implement change or improvement.
Check/ Study	Measure results and compare to plan goals. Results of tested change or improvement are evaluated, and from this step, further action is determined.	Measure effect. Plan successful? Determine next action.
Act	Take corrective action based on results of study. Alternative continued evaluation is required, change or improvement implemented, or another change or improvement is planned.	Standardize change. Document project.

Figure 24   The Deming/Shewhart cycle.

well as be more creative. It was originated by Walter Shewhart in the 1930s and subsequently passed on to Deming before World War II.

One well-known and frequently used model for continuous improvement (kaizen) is referred to as the Deming cycle. Since he learned about it from Dr. Shewhart of AT&T Bell Labs, Dr. Deming called it the Shewhart cycle. However, the name which most completely describes the model is the plan–do–check–act cycle. Later on, Shewhart revised his model to become the plan–do–study–act cycle.

DEPLOYMENT CHART

A deployment chart (or responsibility chart) is a chart, usually an L-shaped matrix, used to identify or clarify deployment/assignment responsibilities. It can also be used to identify the importance of a responsibility or action as well as the flow of actions. In the latter sense, it is similar in purpose to a process map.

A deployment chart can be used within a team setting or with large organizations. It portrays who has what primary and secondary responsibilities and allows for easy verification when an activity has been completed. A slightly more complex version known as an assignment matrix can be used to make assignments based on individual ability and availability.

DESIGN OF EXPERIMENTS

Overview

Design of experiments (DOE) is an organized collection of tools and techniques used to create and evaluate efficient experimentation. One intent of applying DOE is to minimize the assets required to obtain a maximum quantity of much-needed data. The assets include cost, time, and physical resources such as capital equipment, raw materials, and test facilities.

The language of DOE is influenced by its genesis in the scientific, statistical, and engineering communities. Design of experiments does not sound like a production tool. People unfamiliar with the subject might think that DOE sounds like something from research and development. The fact is that DOE is at the heart of a process improvement flow that will help a manufacturing manager obtain what he or she most wants in production—a smooth and efficient operation.

Run	A	B	C	AB	AC	BC	ABC
1	−	−	−	+	+	+	−
2	+	−	−	−	−	+	+
3	−	+	−	−	+	−	+
4	+	+	−	+	−	−	−
5	−	−	+	+	−	−	+
6	+	−	+	−	+	−	−
7	−	+	+	−	−	+	−
8	+	+	+	+	+	+	+
Σ+	4	4	4	4	4	4	4
Σ−	4	4	4	4	4	4	4

− = lower setting or level
+ = upper setting or level

Figure 25　Typical designed experiment.

DOE can appear complicated at first, but many researchers, writers, and software engineers have turned this concept into a useful collection of tools for application in every manufacturing operation. Don't let the idea of an *experiment* turn you away from applying this most useful tool. Well-planned DOEs are carefully structured to efficiently obtain useful information.

DOE is directly applicable to a broad variety of business and industrial applications. It can be effectively applied by the average businessperson with just a bit of technical training (two to three days). A designed experiment is no more than a test or trial program that has been well-structured to accurately measure the results (response or output/dependent variables) in comparison to the inputs (treatments, factors, or input/independent variables). DOE can be the most valuable single set of tools for the optimization and improvement of products, services, and processes.

Figure 25 illustrates a typical designed experiment with three factors, three two-way interactions, and one three-way interaction.

Background

Design of experiments began out of a need to plan very efficient experiments in agriculture in England during the early part of the

20th century. Agriculture poses unique problems for experimentation in that farmers have little control over the quality of soil and no control whatsoever over the weather. This means that a promising new hybrid seed in a field with poor soil could show a reduced yield when compared to the same seed planted in a better soil. Alternatively, weather or soil could cause a new seed to appear better, prompting a costly change for farmers when the results actually stemmed from more favorable growing conditions during the experiment. Although these considerations are more exaggerated for farmers, the same factors affect manufacturing. Manufacturers strive to make operations consistent, but there are slight differences from machine to machine, operator to operator, shift to shift, supplier to supplier, lot to lot, and plant to plant. These and other differences can affect results during experimentation with the introduction of a new material or even a small change in a process, thus leading to incorrect conclusions.

In addition, the long lead time necessary to obtain results in agriculture (the growing season) and to repeat an experiment, if necessary, requires that experiments must be efficient and well planned. After an experiment is started, it is too late to include another factor; it must wait until the next season! This same discipline is useful in manufacturing. You want an experiment to provide the most useful information in the shortest time, so resources (personnel and equipment) can be returned to production.

One of the early pioneers in this field was Sir Ronald Fisher. He developed the initial methodology for separating the experimental variance between the factors and the underlying process and began his experimentation in biology and agriculture. The method he proposed is known today as analysis of variance (ANOVA).

Several alternate DOE approaches have been developed by various statisticians and engineers, each proposing their own particular model and the best solution methodology. Besides Fisher's classical DOE, robust design (originated by Taguchi) and statistical engineering (originated by Shainin) are the most widely used approaches to DOE that apply most directly to management, industrial, service, and administrative processes of concern to business.

Some of the most frequently used DOE tools and techniques are:

- Analysis of variance (ANOVA)

- Confirmation run

- Fractional factorial design

- Full factorial design
- Interaction table
- Orthogonal array
- Pink X shuffle
- Quality loss function
- Rank order significance test
- Refining experiment
- Response curve
- Response surface methodology
- Screening experiment
- Signal to noise ratios

Planning for a DOE

Planning for a DOE is not particularly challenging, but there are some approaches to use that help to avoid potential pitfalls. The first and most important concept is to include many process stakeholders in the planning effort. Ideally, the planning group should include at least one representative from design, production technical support, and production operators. It is not necessary to assemble a large group, but these functions should all be represented during planning meetings.

The rationale for their inclusion is to obtain their input in both the planning and the execution of the experiment. As you can imagine, experiments are not done every day, and communication is necessary to understand the objective, the plan, and the order of execution.

When the planning team is assembled, start by brainstorming the factors that may be included in the experiment. These may be tabulated and then prioritized. One tool that is frequently used for brainstorming factors is a cause-and-effect diagram (a fishbone or Ishikawa diagram). This tool helps prompt the planning team regarding some elements to be considered as experimental factors.

Beginners to DOE may be overly enthusiastic and want to include too many factors in the initial experiment. Although it is desirable to include as many factors as is affordable to determine those that are significant, each factor that is included brings a cost. For example, consider an experiment with five factors, each at two levels. When all the possible combinations are included in the experiment (this is called a full factorial design), the experiment will take $2^5 = 32$ experimental runs to complete each factor-level setting combination just once! Replicating an experiment at least once is desirable. For this experiment, one replication will take 64 runs. In general, if an experiment has k factors at two levels, l factors at three levels, and m factors at four levels, the number of runs to complete every experimental factor level setting is given by $2^k * 3^l * 4^m$. As you can see, the size of the experiment can grow quickly. It is important to prioritize the possible factors for the experiment and include the most significant ones with respect to the time and material that can be devoted to the DOE on the given process.

If it is desirable to experiment with a large number of factors, there are ways to reduce the size of the experiment. Some methods are to reduce the number of factor levels. It is not usually necessary to run factors at greater than three levels. In most cases, responses (the values of the output variables) are linear over the range of experimental values, and two levels are sufficient. As a rule of thumb, it is not necessary to experiment with factors at more than two levels unless the factors are qualitative (material types, suppliers, and so on) or the response is expected to be nonlinear (quadratic, exponential, or logarithmic) due to some known physical phenomenon.

Here's another method to reduce the size of an experiment. A full factorial design is generally desirable because it allows the experimenter to assess not only the significance of each factor but *all* the interactions that exist between the factors. For example, given factors T (temperature), P (pressure), and M (material) in an experiment, a full factorial design can detect the significance of T, P, and M as well as interactions TP, TM, PM, and TPM.

There is, however, a class of experiments where the experimenter deliberately reduces the size of the experiment and gives up some of the resulting potential information by a strategic reduction in factor-level setting combinations. This class is generally called *fractional factorial* experiments because the resulting DOE is a fraction of the full factorial design. For example, a one-half fractional experiment would consist of 2^{n-1} factor level setting combinations. Many fractional factorial designs have been developed so the design gives up (is unable to provide) information on some or all of the potential interactions. (The formal term for this loss of information is *confounding*—the interaction is not lost, it is confounded or mixed with another interaction's or factor's result.)

To use one of these designs, an experimenter should make use of software applications such as MINITAB, JMP, or SPSS. These will have guidance tables or selection options to guide you to a design. In general, employ designs that confound higher-level interactions (three-way, four-way, and so on). Avoid designs that confound individual factors with each other or two-way interactions (*AB, AC,* and so on) and, if possible, use a design that preserves two-way interactions. Most experimental practitioners will tell you that three-way or higher interactions are not often detected and are not usually of engineering significance even if noted.

The next part of planning the experiment is to determine the factor levels. Factor levels will fall into two general categories. Some factors are quantitative and will cover a range of possible settings; temperature is one example. Often these factors are continuous. A subset of this type of factor is one with an ordered set of *levels*. An example of this is high–medium–low fan settings. Some experimental factors are known as attribute or qualitative factors. These include material types, suppliers, operators, and so on. The distinction between these two types of factors really drives the experimental analysis and sometimes the experimental planning. For example, while experimenting with the temperatures 100, 125, and 150°C, a regression could be performed and it could identify the optimum temperature as something between the three experimental settings, 133°C for example. While experimenting with three materials: *A, B,* and *C,* you do not often have the option of selecting a material part way between *A* and *B* if such a material is not on the market!

Regarding factor levels, the attribute factors are generally given. Quantitative factors pose the problem of selecting the levels for the experiment. Generally, the levels should be set wide enough apart to allow identification of differences, but not so wide as to ruin the experiment or cause misleading settings. Consider curing a material at ~100°C. If your oven maintains temperature ±5°C, then an experiment of 95, 100, and 105°C may be a waste of time. At the same time, an experiment of 50, 100, and 150°C may be so broad that the lower temperature material doesn't cure, and the higher temperature material burns. Experimental levels of 90, 100, and 110°C are likely to be more appropriate.

After the experiment is planned, it is important to randomize the order of the runs. Randomization is the key to preventing some environmental factor that changes over time from confounding with an experimental factor. For example, suppose you are experimenting with reducing chatter on a milling machine. You are experimenting with cutting speed and material from two suppliers, A and B. If you run all of A's samples first, would you expect tool wear to affect the output when B is run? Using randomization, the order would be mixed so that each material sample has an equal probability of the application of either a fresh or a dulled cutting edge.

Randomization can be accomplished by sorting on random numbers added to the rows in a spreadsheet. Another method is to add telephone numbers taken sequentially from the phone book to each run and sort the runs by these numbers. You can also draw the numbers from a hat or any other method that removes human bias. Personally, I use a handheld device designed to generate numbers for use in state-run lotteries.

When you conduct an experiment that includes replicates, you may be tempted to randomize the factor-level setting combinations and run the replicates back-to-back while at the combination setting. This is less desirable than full randomization for the reasons previously given. Sometimes, an experiment is difficult to fully randomize due to the nature of experimental elements. For example, an experiment on a heat treat oven or furnace for ceramics may be difficult to fully randomize because of the time involved with changing the oven temperature. In this case, you can relax the randomization somewhat and randomize factor-level combinations while allowing the replicates at each factor-level setting combination to go back-to-back. Randomization can also be achieved by randomizing how material is assigned to the individual runs.

Executing the DOE Efficiently

An experimenter will find it important and useful to assemble all the personnel likely to handle experimental material into the planning at some point for training. Every experimenter has had one or more experiments ruined by someone who didn't understand the objective or significance of the experimental steps. Errors of this sort include mixing the material (not maintaining traceability to the experimental runs), running all the material at the same setting (not changing process setting according to plan), and other instances of Murphy's Law that may enter the experiment. It is also important to train everyone involved with the experiment to write down times, settings, and variances that may be observed. The latter might include maintenance performed on a process during the experiment, erratic gage readings, shift changes, power losses, and so on. The astute experimenter must also recognize that when an operator makes errors, you can't berate the operator and expect cooperation on the next trial of the experiment. Everyone involved will know what happened, and the next time there is a problem with your experiment, you'll be the last to know exactly what went wrong!

Glossary of DOE Terms and Acronyms

confounding—When a design is used that does not explore all the factor-level setting combinations, some interactions may be mixed with each other or with experimental factors such that the analysis cannot tell which factor contributes to or influences the magnitude of the response effect. When responses from interactions/factors are mixed, they are said to be *confounded*.

DOE—Design of experiments is also known as industrial experiments, experimental design, and design of industrial experiments.

factor—A process setting or input to a process. For example, the temperature setting on an oven is a factor as well as the type of raw material used.

factor-level settings—The combinations of factors and their settings for one or more runs of the experiment. For example, consider an experiment in three factors, each with two levels (*H* and *L* = high and low). The possible factor level settings are: *H–H–H, H–L–L,* and so on.

factor space—The hypothetical space determined by the extremes of all the factors considered in the experiment. If there are *k* factors in the experiment, the factor space is *k*-dimensional.

interaction—Factors are said to have an interaction when changes in one factor cause an increased or reduced response to changes in another factor or factors.

randomization—After an experiment is planned, the order of the runs is randomized. This reduces the effect of uncontrolled changes in the environment such as tool wear, chemical depletion, warm-up, and so on.

repetition—When each factor level setting combination is run more than one time, the experiment is *repeated*. Each run beyond the first one for a factor level setting combination is a *repetition*.

replication—When an experiment is duplicated by other operators, on different equipment, at other times, and/or in a different plant, the experiment is *replicated*. Thus, *replication* is an attempt to reproduce the original experiment and obtain the same results.

response—The result to be measured and improved by the experiment. In most experiments there is one response, but it is certainly possible to be concerned about more than one response.

statistically significant—A factor or interaction is said to be statistically significant if its contribution to the variance of the experiment appears to be larger than would be expected from the normal variance of the process.

DESIGN FOR MANUFACTURE AND ASSEMBLY (DFMA)

Design for manufacture and assembly (DFMA) is a modern technique for the development of new products. It ensures high product quality while maintaining minimum manufacturing costs. The major benefit of using DFMA is achieved by assuring that the desired design features are incorporated while minimizing the cost of manufacture and assembly. This is accomplished by treating manufacture and assembly requirements as product design requirements.

DFMA begins with the selection of a cross-functional team. The team members should as a rule include representatives from all manufacturing and assembly operations, design engineering, quality, material, and manufacturing engineering. The team begins by evaluating the manufacturing/assembly processes for a proposed product design. This evaluation is used to improve the design so as to streamline the manufacturing/assembly processes. Depending on the nature of the product being evaluated, a DFMA workshop would be expected to seek and achieve the following goals:

- Reduce the number and types of fasteners required.

- Minimize the number of settings and adjustments.

- Maximize use of snap-on and snap-together techniques.

- Make a minimum number of parts serve multiple purposes.

- Add features to prevent improper assembly (poka-yoke).

- Make parts self-aligning.

- Design for symmetry.

- Develop an efficient and effective manufacturing/assembly process flow.

- Use gravity to assist parts flow and assembly.

ERROR/MISTAKE-PROOFING
(POKA-YOKE)

Originally known in Japan as *baka-yoke* (providing protection from crazy or foolish persons), error-proofing or *poka-yoke* (pronounced POH-kah YOH-kay) is a means to provide *fail-safe* protection from human errors. There are many types of error-proofing in the form of simple machine or process revisions and modifications as well as product variations and retrofits. The following are examples of error-proofing at various levels.

Basic Error-Proofing

- Use cross-checking when totaling a number of columns.

- Write down instructions to employees for their future reference.

- Increase the effectiveness of internal communications. Ask employees to repeat instructions to ensure understanding.

Intermediate Error-Proofing

- Use different color paper for different purposes. This helps ensure that correspondence is directed to the correct location.

- Make certain that on/off switches on PCs are physically distanced from other switches or buttons on the PCs, so they are not accidentally turned off, resulting in a loss of data or information.

- Put all letters in envelopes with plastic windows to display names and addresses already typed on the letters. This eliminates retyping names and addresses as well as having letters sent to the wrong persons.

Advanced Error-Proofing

- When using polarized electrical equipment, use electrical plugs that can only be inserted into the proper sockets. This is accomplished by making one of the plug inserts wider or narrower than the other.

- When using machinery that can potentially injure its operator, incorporate safety features into the operational design of the machine so that necessary guards must be in place before the machine can function.

- When starting an automobile, it could accidentally move in an unexpected direction with disastrous results. To eliminate the potential for such events, incorporate a safety feature that prevents starting a vehicle and putting it into gear without first depressing the brake pedal.

Figure 26 presents some examples of how error-proofing has been successfully employed.

Figure 26   Five popular mistake-proofing techniques.   *continued*

continued

Figure 26   Five popular mistake-proofing techniques.

EVENTS LOG

The sole purpose of an events log is to relieve process operators and support personnel, such as engineers and supervisors, from the necessity of recalling process changes when defects and/or excessive variability are detected. The detection may come about as a result of using control charts, Pareto analysis, and/or histograms.

Events logs were created in response to demonstrated needs for process status documentation. Entries in an events log should be made by any process-related personnel whenever process changes involve the five *M*s and an *E* (men/women, methods, measurement, machine, material, and environment).

Date	Time	Event	Entry By
11-21	8:15 am	Mary in for John	JR
	10:40 am	Begin lot 7P	JR
	1:05 pm	Insert new tooling	MS
	2:37 pm	Start new procedure	MS

Figure 27   Events log.

Events log entries are analyzed whenever control chart, Pareto diagram, or histogram data indicate significant alterations to process output, whether good or bad. The contents of a typical events log are shown in Figure 27.

F

FAILURE MODE AND EFFECTS ANALYSIS (FMEA)

The failure mode and effects analysis (FMEA) is widely recognized as a valuable reliability tool. The FMEA specifically determines what can go wrong with each individual piece of hardware and what effects each failure can cause. It is primarily used for doing subsystem and system hazard analyses.

It is used to provide failure-focused data relative to reliability, maintainability, and systems safety. The FMEA evaluates both product and process reliability; it also identifies single-point failures. It can be performed at various levels of inquiry and at different times in the product lifecycle.

There are two forms of FMEA: functional and hardware. Functional FMEA is a top-level evaluation tool used early in a program to examine ways in which subsystems can fail and the effect of these failures on the system or subsystems. Hardware FMEA is the more commonly used form and focuses on the use of detailed design information relative to assemblies, subassemblies, and components.

Failure mode and effects analysis takes a system or a subsystem, breaks it down into individual assemblies, subassemblies, and components, and then systematically looks at the different ways each component could fail as well as the effects of each failure on both the immediate assembly and, eventually, the entire system or subsystem. Whenever it is available, the effort includes quantified reliability data (see Figure 28).

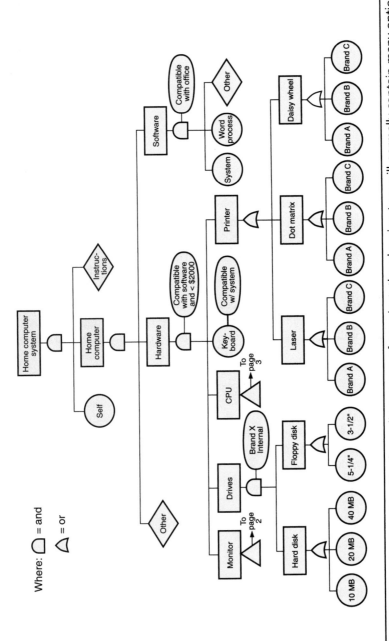

Figure 28 Planning tree. Used in the earliest stages of a project, the planning tree will normally contain many options indicated by the *or* gates.

Analytical trees are frequently used as feeder documents for the FMEA. Using relevant information generated by the FMEA, outputs from an FMEA can include a critical items list (CIL), stand-alone hazard analysis reports, and subsystem or system hazard analysis reports.

FAULT TREE ANALYSIS (FTA)

Fault tree analysis (FTA) was developed by the Bell Telephone Laboratories for the U.S. Air Force in 1962. It is a highly detailed analytical technique used to determine the various ways in which specific types of system defects could occur. FTA is based on the use of a negative analytical tree.

There are two primary approaches to FTA: the qualitative approach and the quantitative approach. The qualitative approach uses deductive logic (inferring from a generally accepted principle to a particular event) to determine the combination of lower-level events that could result in the occurrence of a specific, undesired top-level event. This information is then used to evaluate both the overall likelihood of occurrence and the methods used to reduce it. The quantitative approach adds reliability or failure data to achieve the same objective.

Fault tree analysis is especially valuable for systematically reducing the probability of an undesired event. An FTA requires the direct involvement of a skilled, knowledgeable analyst as well as a great deal of time to conduct the analysis, especially if the project is complex and the quantitative approach is necessary.

The primary advantages of an FTA are that it produces meaningful data used for evaluating and improving the overall reliability of a system, and it evaluates the effectiveness of and the need for redundancy within the system (see Figure 29).

As with any tool or technique, FTA has limitations. The undesired event to be evaluated must be foreseen and all significant contributors to system failure must be anticipated. The FTA effort can be quite time-consuming and, as a direct result, more expensive than lesser types of analysis. Its level of success depends to a great extent upon the skills of the lead analyst.

Fault tree analysis is primarily employed as a tool for conducting system or subsystem hazard analyses. This is true despite the fact that qualitative or top-level analyses (those with a limited number of tiers or detail) can be used to perform preliminary hazard analyses.

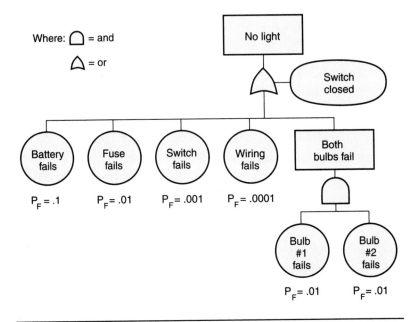

Figure 29   Fault tree.

Generally, an FTA is applied to analyze critical item failures that were previously identified using a failure mode and effects analysis or some other type of hazard analysis. FTAs are also used to analyze other undesirable events capable of producing catastrophic or otherwise unacceptable losses.

FIVE S (5S)

The original 5S principles were stated in Japanese. Because of their proven value to western industry, they have been translated and restated in English. The 5S is a mantra of sorts designed to help build a quality work environment, both physically and mentally.

The 5S condition of a work area is critical to the morale of employees and the basis of customers' first impressions. Management's attitude regarding their employees is reflected in the 5S condition of the work area. The 5S philosophy applies in any work area. The elements of 5S are simple to learn and important to implement:

- *Sort.* Eliminate whatever is not needed.

- *Straighten.* Organize whatever remains.

- *Shine.* Clean the work area.

- *Standardize.* Schedule regular cleaning and maintenance.

- *Sustain.* Make 5S a way of life.

There are numerous benefits to be derived from implementing 5S:

- Improved safety

- Higher equipment availability

- Lower defect rates

- Reduced costs

- Increased production agility and flexibility

- Improved employee morale

- Better asset utilization

- Enhanced enterprise image to customers, suppliers, employees, and management

Figure 30 is an example of a 5S workplace scan diagnostic checklist.

Category	Item	Rating Level					Remarks
		L0	L1	L2	L3	L4	
Sort (Organization)	Distinguish between what is needed and not needed						
	Unneeded equipment, tools, furniture, and so on, are present						
	Unneeded items are on walls, bulletin boards, and so on						
	Items are present in aisles, stairways, corners, and so on						
	Unneeded inventory, supplies, arts, or materials are present						
	Safety hazards (water, oil, chemical, machines) exist						
Set in Order (Orderliness)	A place for everything, and everything in its place						
	Correct places for items are not obvious						
	Items are not in their places						

Number of problems	Rating level
3 or more	Level 0 (L0)
3–4	Level 1 (L1)
2	Level 2 (L2)
1	Level 3 (L3)
None	Level 4 (L4)

Figure 30 Five S workplace scan diagnostic checklist. *continued*

continued

Category	Item	Rating Level					Remarks
		L0	**L1**	**L2**	**L3**	**L4**	
Set in Order (Orderliness)	Aisles, workstations, equipment locations are not indicated						
	Items are not put away immediately after use						
	Height and quantity limits are not obvious						
Shine (Cleanliness)	Cleaning and looking for ways to keep it clean and organized						
	Floors, walls, stairs, and surfaces are not free of dirt, oil, and grease						
	Equipment is not kept clean and free of dirt, oil, and grease						
	Cleaning materials are not easily accessible						
	Lines, labels, signs, and so on are not clean and unbroken						
	Other cleaning problems of any kind are present						
Standardize (Adherence)	Maintain and monitor the first three categories						
	Necessary information is not visible						
	All standards are not known and visible						
	Checklists don't exist for cleaning and maintenance jobs						
	All quantities and limits are not easily recognizable						
	How many items can't be located in 30 seconds?						
Sustain (Self-Discipline)	Stick to the rules						
	How many workers have not had 5S training?						
	How many times, last week, was daily 5S not performed?						
	Number of times that personal belongings are not neatly stored						
	Number of times job aids are not available or up-to-date						
	Number of times, last week, daily 5S inspections not performed						
	TOTAL						

Figure 30 Five S workplace scan diagnostic checklist.

FIVE WHYS

The *five whys* is a technique for discovering the root cause (or causes) of a problem by repeatedly asking the question "why?" Five is an arbitrary figure. You never know exactly how many times you'll have to ask "why." The five whys technique helps identify the root causes of a problem and how different causes of a problem might be related

To begin, the problem should be described in very specific terms. Then, ask why it happens. If the answer doesn't identify a root cause, then ask "why" again. The root cause has been identified when asking "why" doesn't provide any more useful information. Continue asking "why" until the root causes have been identified.

Remember, always focus on the process aspects of a problem rather than on the persons involved. Finding scapegoats doesn't solve problems!

Here's an example. A program office wants to find out why they missed their initial operating capability (IOC) date.

We missed our IOC!

Why?　Our contract delivery schedule slipped.

Why?　There were a lot of engineering changes.

Why?　The contractor didn't understand our initial requirements.

Why?　Our technical data package wasn't prepared very well.

Why?　We only took one week to prepare it.

At this point, the group recognized poor requirements planning as a root cause of the problem. As a result, the group decided to allow more time up front in the planning process for requirements analysis.

Suppose you hear the following statement: "We used to have a respectable defect rate; it ran about 100 ppm. Then, a few months ago, it jumped up to about 2000 ppm." Using the five whys technique, the subsequent discussion might go something like this:

Q:　Do you have any ideas why the big increase in the defect rate?

A: I'm not sure, but it could be a couple of things. For example, it might be the materials that our new supplier is sending us, or it could be the higher conveyor speeds that we're running on the line in order to meet the new production goals.

Q: What do you think it is?

A: I think it might be a combination of the new materials and the higher conveyor speeds.

Q: Why do you think that's the reason for the higher defect rates?

A: Well, we used to run higher speeds on a job we had a few years ago, and from time to time, the defect rate would jump up and then come back. We were never absolutely sure why.

Q: How about the new materials? Why do you think that they may be contributing to the increase of the defect rate?

A: Its nothing official yet, but we've heard that the new supplier has been cutting corners and the quality of the materials we've been receiving from them is questionable.

Q: That all sounds pretty interesting, but why do you think that it might be a combination of the material quality and the higher conveyor speeds?

A: It's the timing. The defect rate didn't really jump up when the conveyor speeds increased, but it did when the new materials entered the line.

Q: What can we do to find out for sure?

A: We can use a design of experiments to figure out if the interaction between the new materials and the conveyor speeds is really why the defect rates have increased.

Ask "why" five times to determine the root cause.

1. Why is this machine not running? Because its drive belt is broken.

2. Why is its drive belt broken? Because the drive gear was not turning fast enough.

3. Why was the drive gear not turning fast enough? Because the drive shaft's lubrication reservoir ran empty.

4. Why did the drive shaft's lubrication reservoir run empty? Because the PM for this machine is overdue by almost two weeks.

5. Why is the preventive maintenance (PM) for this machine overdue by almost two weeks? Because the lubrication maintenance person is on a two-week vacation.

6. Why didn't someone else cover for the lubrication maintenance person during his vacation? Because we do not have a vacation coverage plan for the maintenance department, and operators are not trained and empowered to do lubrication.

Sometimes you have to ask "why" more than five times to get to the root cause.

FOCUS GROUPS

Depending on their intent or purpose, focus groups take on various faces, much like a social or cultural chameleon. Focus groups are a powerful means to evaluate products and services or test new ideas. Basically, focus groups are collective interviews of six to ten people at the same time in the same place. An organization can obtain a great deal of information during a focus group session.

A focus group is a structured but informal technique to assess customer needs and feelings. In a focus group, customers and potential customers are brought together to discuss issues and concerns about products, services, or ideas. The group typically lasts about two hours and is conducted by a facilitator who maintains the group's focus.

Focus groups bring out users' spontaneous reactions and ideas and permit observation of some group dynamics and organizational issues. Participants are asked to discuss how they perform activities that span many days or weeks, which is something that is expensive to observe directly. However, an organization can only assess what customers say they do and not the way customers actually operate a product or use a service. Since there are often major differences between what people say and what they do, direct observation of individual users is sometimes necessary to supplement focus groups.

For participants, the focus group session should feel free-flowing and relatively unstructured but in reality the facilitator must follow a preplanned script of specific issues and set goals for the type of information to be gathered. During the focus group session, its leader has the difficult job of keeping the discussion on track without inhibiting the flow of ideas and comments. He or she must also insure that all focus group members contribute to the discussion and must avoid letting one participant's opinions dominate the discussion.

After the session, data analysis can be as simple as having the facilitator write a short report summing up the prevailing mood in the focus group, sometimes illustrated with a few meaningful quotes. Figure 31 is a checklist for focus groups.

Preparing for session:

1. Identify the major objectives.
2. Develop specific questions.
3. Plan the session.
4. Contact potential participants with an invitation to attend.
5. Remind participants about three days in advance of the session.

Developing questions:

1. Carefully develop five to six questions.
2. Facilitator examines major topic for discussion.
3. Focus groups are collective interviews.

Planning the session:

1. Scheduling
2. Meeting place and refreshments
3. Ground rules
4. Agenda

Figure 31 Focus group checklist.

continued

continued

5. Membership

6. Media for recording session

Facilitating the session:

1. Major goal to collect useful information

2. Introductions

3. Explain media used for recording session

4. Carry out agenda

5. Carefully state each question

6. After hearing answers, summarize what was said

7. Ensure even participation

8. Close the session

Following the session:

1. Check recording media for functionality.

2. Review meeting notes for clarity.

3. Write any noteworthy observations based on session content.

Figure 31   Focus group checklist.

FORCE ANALYSIS

Force analysis is a graphic method of identifying external and internal forces at work. It is used as a tool to assist in the development of organizational contingency plans.

Force analysis is presented as a circle with the external forces portrayed as arrows on the outside and pointed inwardly, while internal forces are portrayed as arrows on the inside and pointed outwardly (see Figure 32).

The external forces are those that are perceived as being in opposition to the plan or objective. The internal forces are those that are viewed as supportive of accomplishing the plan or objective.

The length of each arrow on both sides of the circumference designates the anticipated relative strength of that force.

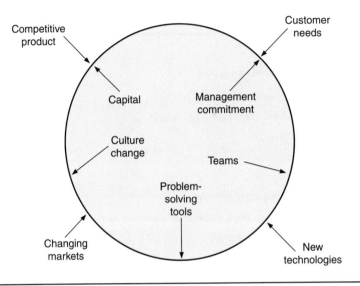

Figure 32   Example of a force analysis.

FORCED CHOICE

Forced choice is used by teams to compare the items in a list based on an agreed-upon standard. Typically, this standard is a value judgment selected by group consensus.

Some possible standards include cost, quality, time, and the like. The list of items may be generated by brainstorming or mind mapping. Using forced choice results in the identification of contradictions in logic as well as in prioritization of the list using pairwise ranking (see Figure 33).

Using a standard question such as, "Which is more expensive, item 1 or item 2," helps to maintain consistency in the comparison process. If this technique seems familiar to you, it may be because this is how an eye doctor determines the extent of need for glasses.

FORCE-FIELD ANALYSIS

Force-field analysis visually identifies the relationships of those significant and opposing forces that influence the achievement of an objective or completion of a plan. Force-field analysis can be used in the following instances:

The chosen standard is *least cost.*

Alternative one	////	4
Alternative two	//	2
Alternative three	/	1
Alternative four		0
Alternative X	///	3

Typical question:
Which costs less, alternative . . . or alternative . . . ?

The result shows alternative one costs less than the other alternatives, and alternative four costs the most.

Figure 33   Example application of forced choice.

- To identify key factors or forces that either promote or hinder desired accomplishments

- To identify improvement opportunities

- To select the best choice from several alternatives

This deceptively simple technique begins with a written statement of the objective or plan that is agreed to by the participants. This is followed by the establishment of a vertical line that separates positive forces on the left of the line and negative forces on the right. Each force is portrayed as a straight horizontal line with the arrowhead of the positive force lines pointed to the right and touching the vertical line and the arrowhead of the negative force lines pointed to the left and touching the vertical line. Wherever a positive force line and a negative force line are in direct opposition to each other, the arrowheads should touch (see Figure 34).

There are two approaches to dealing with the importance or strength of each force. In one approach, the length of each force line, positive or negative, should designate the anticipated relative strength of that force. This provides a clear, unambiguous visualization of the forces with which an organization is dealing.

In the second approach the participants use a one (least) to five (most) scale as the basis for making a collective decision regarding the importance or strength of each force. Use the median to select a single value for each force. For example, suppose five participants

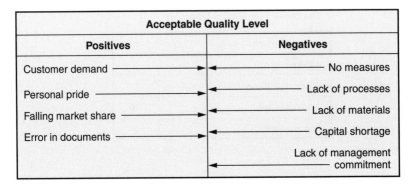

Figure 34 Force-field analysis—without quantification.

offered their individual evaluations as *5, 5, 4, 2,* and *1.* In this case, since the data set contains five values, the value *4* would be selected as the median because there are two values above it (*5* and *5*) and two values below it (*2* and *1*).

After each force has been quantified, all the values of the positive forces are summed, as are the values of the negative forces. The next step is to develop a net value by combining the positives and the negatives.

In comparing three alternatives or choices using force-field analysis, at this point there are three net values. The final step is to rank the alternatives from the greatest net value (first choice) to the least (last choice).

GANTT CHART

A Gantt chart is a horizontal bar chart that was originally developed during World War I for planning and controlling military projects. Today, it is widely used in the planning and managing of projects.

A Gantt chart uses two dimensions. The vertical axis lists the various steps or activities for a project beginning with the first step at the top and the final step at the bottom. The horizontal axis shows the passage of time measured in whatever time units are appropriate.

A Gantt chart uses horizontal bars to depict the planned and actual start and finish times for each step or activity (see Figure 35).

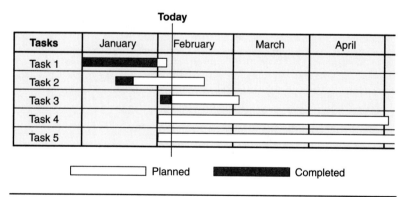

Figure 35   Typical Gantt chart.

The current status of the project is annotated for periodic reviews by participants, management, and/or customers.

In its original design, a Gantt chart did not portray precedence relationships between the steps or activities. This shortcoming led to the development of the critical path method (CPM) and the program evaluation and review technique (PERT) in the 1950s in the United States, and the activity network diagram (AND) in the 1980s in Japan.

GAP ANALYSIS

A gap analysis is an evaluation or comparison of an existing situation, the *as is* condition, against a desired situation, the *should be* condition. This information is then used to determine a course of action to achieve the desired state.

Rather than attempt to examine the entire existing situation, a gap analysis begins with a stratification of the various critical attributes of the *should be* condition. This is followed by a measurement of the *as is* condition against the attributes established as the desired state. Finally, an intervention or corrective action is determined as are the resources necessary to achieve the desired state for each attribute that does not meet the desired state (see Figure 36).

The first step in gap analysis identifies the process performance measure. The second step identifies both your company's performance and the performance of the benchmarking partner involved in the study. Figure 37 is simplified to show a two-company comparison;

Attributes	Desired State	Existing State	Gap	Action to Close Gap	Resources Required to Close Gap

Figure 36   Gap analysis matrix.

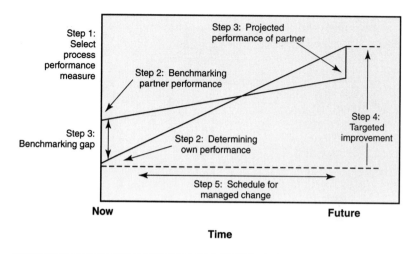

Figure 37 Process contributions to developing and closing.

three, four, or five companies can be involved in a study. The third step indicates not only the magnitude of the performance gap between your company and the leading company at the current time but also the performance trend of the leading company as projected to the planning horizon and, thus, the magnitude of improvement necessary for your company to become the benchmark for this process relative to its partner company.

HEURISTIC REDEFINITION

Redefining a problem and understanding it as a system are useful approaches to finding a solution to a problem. Heuristic redefinition can help a team visualize the various elements of a problem as well as its underlying structure.

Heuristic redefinition is a two-step macroprocess that begins by creating a visual presentation of a problem. This is followed by a systematic evaluation to search for the optimal solution to the problem. Development of a visual presentation is encouraged. It is accomplished by having a team draw a picture of the overall system as well as symbols or icons for the most important components of the problem. The visualization process clarifies the problem as a system because the resulting picture reveals system components, its subsystems, and interrelationships expressed in terms of a specified goal.

Potential concerns, articulated as questions, are formed based on these interrelationships. The questions are systematically evaluated using a prioritization matrix where the likelihood of success, the effort needed, and the quality of the result of each are noted. Finally, the team discusses which concern is best suited in terms of success, opportunities, and/or innovations.

This approach to problem solving involves drawing a symbolic picture of the problem and then listing the different parts of the system. The final step is to construct a prioritization matrix for use in selecting the one or two ways of looking at the problem that are most likely to assist the team in achievement of its goal.

HIDDEN FACTORY

The hidden factory is that portion of the total capacity of an organization that exists for the following purposes: to rework or touch up unsatisfactory parts, to replace products recalled from the field, to retest and reinspect rejected units, and to store unsatisfactory and rejected goods until they can be reworked, touched up, retested, reinspected, or disposed of.

Based on available data, it has been estimated that the hidden factory can be 15 to 40 percent of the productive capacity of an enterprise (see Figure 38). There is no better way to improve productivity than to convert the hidden factory to productive use; enterprisewide continuous improvement programs provide one of the most practical ways to accomplish this objective. Figure 39 provides insight regarding how the hidden factory is positioned with respect to the overall supply chain process.

In the mid-1980s, while I was the senior statistician for a manufacturing division of a major aerospace firm, I shared the concept of the hidden factory with a training class composed entirely of senior and middle management. When I noted the 15 to 40 percent hidden factory statistic with the class, one of the class members vociferously denied that such a figure was possible. He said he was going to have an audit conducted of his engineering division to determine the proportion of the resources and facilities under his control that was hidden factory. He said that it might be as high as five percent, but no higher.

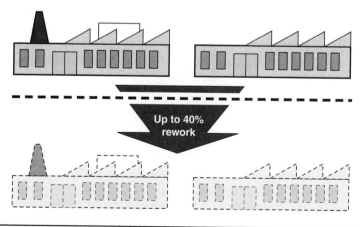

Figure 38   The "hidden factory."

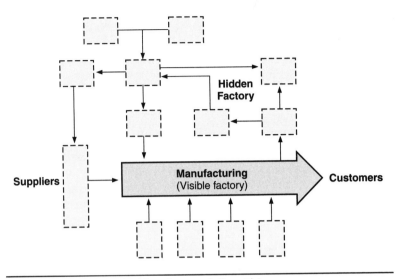

Figure 39 Where a hidden factory falls within a process.

Later, I was invited to attend a senior staff meeting composed of the president, vice presidents, directors, senior managers, and the division manager from my class. He explained to everyone in the conference room what I had claimed about the extent of the negative impact of the hidden factory. Then he described his disbelief and the audit of his engineering division. He then admitted to his colleagues the surprising results of the audit. Fully 33 percent of the personnel, resources, equipment, material, and facilities under his management were regularly committed to doing things right other than the first time, that is, the hidden factory. This was a major admission in the presence of his peers.

What proportion of your area of responsibility is hidden factory? And what are you going to do about it?

HISTOGRAM

Description

A histogram is a graphic representation of the distribution of variable data (data generated by taking measurements) using a bar chart. It is commonly used to visually communicate information about a process or a product and help make decisions regarding prioritization of improvement initiatives.

This information is represented by a series of columns of varying heights (see Figure 40). The columns are of equal width because they all represent a specific interval with an equal range of observations. Column height is a function of the number of observations within the interval covered by each column. Thus, column height varies according to the number of hits within a specified interval.

With most naturally occurring data, there is a tendency for many observations to occur toward the center of the distribution (known in statistical circles as the *central tendency*) with progressively fewer points occurring further from the center.

Histograms offer a quick look at data at a single point in time (for the last hour, last shift, last day). They do not display variation or trends over time. A histogram displays how the cumulative data looks for a specified period of time. It is useful in understanding the relative frequencies (percentages) or frequency (quantity) of the data and how that data is distributed.

Many candidate processes or products for improvement can be identified using this one basic tool. The frequency and shape of

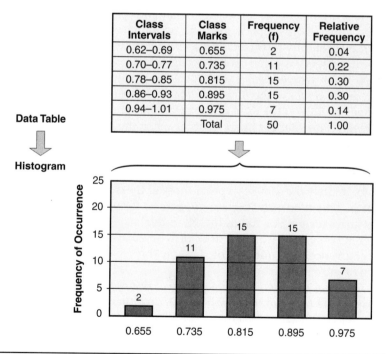

Data Table

Class Intervals	Class Marks	Frequency (f)	Relative Frequency
0.62–0.69	0.655	2	0.04
0.70–0.77	0.735	11	0.22
0.78–0.85	0.815	15	0.30
0.86–0.93	0.895	15	0.30
0.94–1.01	0.975	7	0.14
	Total	50	1.00

Histogram

Figure 40 Histograms.

the data distribution provide insights that would not be apparent from data tables (check sheets) alone. Histograms also form the basis for two other frequently used Six Sigma/TQM/CI tools: Pareto analysis, and process capability analysis.

Types of Histograms

Useful information about a population can be obtained by examining the shape and spread of a histogram constructed from either sampling or census data drawn from the population. There are many typical shapes, each with its own subset of possible spreads of the data. Here are several combinations of common histogram shapes and spreads:

Normal (symmetrical or bell-shaped). The mean, median, and mode are all of approximately the same value and located in the center of the range of data. The frequency of occurrence is the greatest in the center and gradually lessens toward the skirts or tails of the distribution of the data.

Positive skew (asymmetrical). The mean value is located to the left of the center of the range of data. The frequency of occurrence declines rapidly to the left of the mean and gradually to the right of the mean. This shape is likely to occur when the lower limit is either theoretically restricted by a specification value or when values less than a specific value cannot occur.

Negative skew (asymmetrical). The mean value is located to the right of the center of the range of data. The frequency of occurrence declines rapidly to the right of the mean and gradually to the left of the mean. This shape is likely to occur when the upper limit is either theoretically restricted by a specification value or when values greater than a certain value cannot occur.

Plateau (rectangular). The frequency of occurrence in each class is approximately the same except for those at the extremes of the range of data. This type of histogram appears to form a plateau or mesa. This shape can occur naturally when dealing with the number of different types of cards in a deck or when counting the frequency of occurrence of a number of dots on the face of a single die or faces of multiple dice.

Twin peak (bimodal). The frequency of occurrence is low near the center of the range of data with a peak on either side. This shape is known to occur when two frequency distributions with quite different mean values are mixed together.

Construction

How to construct a histogram is best explained using an example. Suppose that a process improvement team collects a random sample composed of 70 data points ($n = 70$) and that the greatest value is 120 ($X_{max} = 120$) and the smallest value is 80 ($X_{min} = 80$). The first step is to determine the range (R) which is mathematically defined as $R = X_{max} - X_{min}$. In this case, $R = 120 - 80 = 40$.

The second step is to determine the number of columns in the histogram. This is done by taking the square root of the number of data points (in this example, $n = 70$). If you're seeing this for the first time, you're probably thinking, "Where did that come from?" There is no scientific basis for this technique, but it's time tested and it works, so bear with me. The number of columns in a histogram is important because, if there are too few or too many, you don't really gain an understanding of the true shape or profile of the frequency distribution of the data that has been collected. Taking the square root of the sample size provides a useful guideline as to the appropriate number of columns to use. In this case, the square root of 70 is between 8 ($8^2 = 64$) and 9 ($9^2 = 81$), so the number of columns in the histogram will be in that general area.

The third step is to calculate the size of the class intervals (CI) in the histogram. To complete this step, divide the range by the square root of the sample size. For this example, divide R (40) by the square root of n (8 since it evenly divides into 40). Since 40 divided by 8 = 5, this is our class interval, that is, the range of data for a single class.

The fourth step is to develop the full range of class intervals, each with a class size of 5.

As is traditional, start with the smallest value, $X_{min} = 80$, and proceed to the largest value, $X_{max} = 120$, in increments equal to the class interval of 5 as follows.

The fifth step is to create a tally sheet. Since this is a simulated example, create a frequency of occurrence figure for each class, as shown in Figure 41.

The sixth and final step is to develop the histogram, which appears in Figure 42.

As noted, be careful not to use too many or too few classes. Either choice can disguise the true frequency distribution of your sampling data, as Figures 43 through 45 demonstrate.

Class Number	Class Interval	Simulated Tally Marks	Frequency of Occurrence
1	81–85	///	3
2	86–90	7H/	5
3	91–95	7H/ ///	8
4	96–100	7H/ 7H/ 7H/ /	16
5	101–105	7H/ 7H/ 7H/ ///	18
6	106–110	7H/ ////	9
7	111–115	7H/ /	6
8	116–120	7H/	5
			Total = 70

Figure 41   Tally sheet.

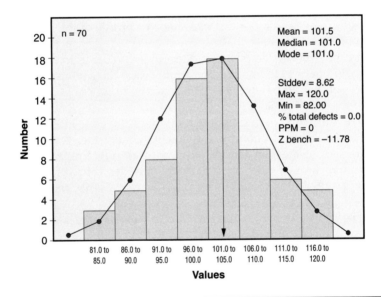

Figure 42   Histogram with correct number of classes.

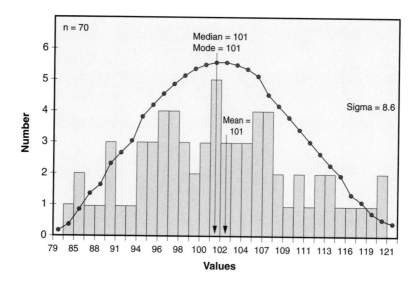

Figure 43 Too many classes.

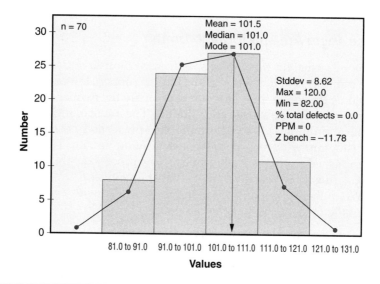

Figure 44 Too few classes (4).

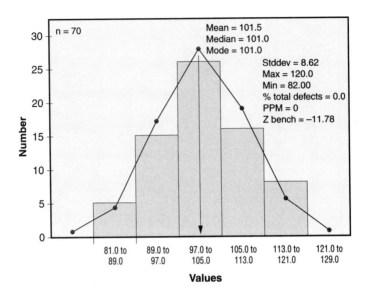

Figure 45   Too few classes (5).

When There Are Specification Limits

It is not unusual for there to be specification limits associated with a histogram. When this occurs, the limits (upper, lower, or both) should be drawn on the histogram to compare the frequency distribution curve with the specification limit(s). The intent of including the specification limit(s) is to determine the spread and positioning of the histogram with respect to the specification limit(s). This can be accomplished mathematically using C_P (the process capability index) and C_{PK} (the mean sensitive process capability index).

When there are specification limits associated with a histogram, any of the following situations can occur:

1. When the histogram satisfies the specification limit(s):

   a. Maintenance of the existing process is sufficient unless there is a compelling need for continuous improvement (see Figure 46).

   b. The specification limits are marginally satisfied; however, there is no room for a shifting of the mean or an increase in the standard deviation (see Figure 47).

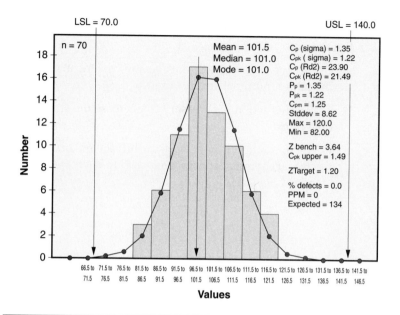

Figure 46 Specification limits—case 1a.

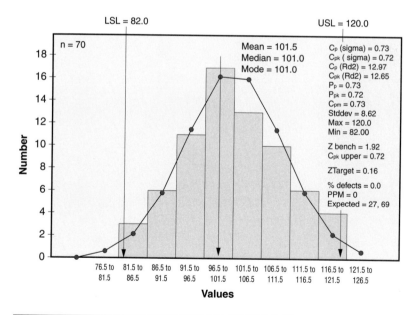

Figure 47 Specification limits—case 1b.

2. When the histogram does not satisfy the specification limit(s):

   a. Corrective action is necessary to shift the mean closer to the target/nominal specification.

   b. Corrective action is necessary to decrease the standard deviation.

   c. Corrective action is necessary to shift the mean closer to the target/nominal specification and to decrease the standard deviation.

IMAGINEERING

Imagineering begins with a team using a process flowchart or a process map of an actual process (see Figure 48). This is commonly referred to as the *as is* model. The team follows with a detailed development of the approach to be taken for the ideal or optimum process, the *should be* model.

When the two flowcharts are compared, the critical differences become much clearer. Then the team asks questions such as "How can these differences be eliminated?" and "How can the process be streamlined?"

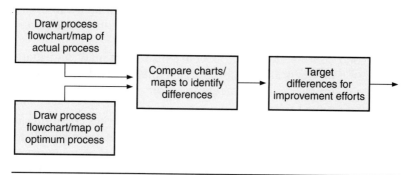

Figure 48   How imagineering is done.

Perhaps there is a task being performed by each of two different departments that could be more efficiently handled by only one, or there might be tasks that run in sequence that could better be done concurrently. In fact, there could be other tasks that, as a result of a process analysis, should not be done at all if the analysis revealed that these tasks add no value to the final product or service.

The same approach can be taken with a product. In this case, the team would begin by asking for a description of the ideal product. Then the team would ask about the differences between the ideal and the actual product. Finally, the team would ask how the product design could be changed to generate an optimal product more likely to please the customer. (See *quality function deployment* and *customer table.*)

INTEGRATED PRODUCT AND PROCESS DEVELOPMENT (IPPD)

Integrated product and process development (IPPD) is not a totally new development or activity. Its roots are in concurrent/simultaneous engineering, and it employs a variety of tools and techniques associated with total quality management (TQM), continuous improvement (CI), and Six Sigma. IPPD is an approach that systematically employs a teaming of various functional disciplines to integrate and concurrently apply all necessary tools and methodologies to produce an effective and efficient product that satisfies customer needs at the right time and place as well as at the right price.

The results of a sound IPPD implementation come from three major areas. First, IPPD is customer-oriented. The entire integrated product and process development team (IPT) must be aware of all customer requirements and what personal contributions are necessary to fulfill these requirements.

Second, results stem from concurrent development and management of products and processes. For a totally new design, an IPT can avoid design iterations stemming from producibility changes following product release.

Third, a well-trained, experienced IPT with good communication skills and well-defined responsibilities can react more quickly to change than can separate functional organizations. The *white spaces* in organizational charts are barriers to efficient communication and timely, multifunctional responses.

The major goals of an IPT and their parallel design activities are given in Figure 49.

IPT Goals	Parallel Design Activities
Shorter time to market	Quality function deployment Design for manufacture and assembly Design for testability Cycle time management
Lower product development costs	Robust design Design for manufacture and assembly Cycle time management
Greater quality	Robust design Design for testability Cycle time management
Lower manufacturing costs	Robust design Design for testability Design for manufacture and assembly Cycle time management
Reduced service costs	Cost of quality Design for compliance Design for serviceability
Enhanced competitiveness	Quality function deployment Improved profit margin Design for performance Cycle time management

Figure 49   Major goals of an IPT.

INTERRELATIONSHIP DIGRAPH (ID)

The relationships among communication data elements are not linear; in fact, they are often multidirectional. In other words, an idea, a concept, an issue, or an action can affect more than one other idea, concept, issue, or action, and the magnitudes of these effects can and do vary. Additionally, the relationships are often hidden and/or not clearly understood.

The interrelationship digraph (ID) is an effective tool for clarifying the relationships between ideas, concepts, issues, or actions. This is accomplished by mapping the cause and effect linkages, that is, the sequential connections among them. The usual input for an ID is the output or result generated from using other tools such as affinity analysis, brainstorming, cause-and-effect analysis, or tree diagrams. The ID can, however, be used to analyze a set of ideas, concepts, issues, or actions generated without first using another tool.

IDs are used in the following cases: when root causes must be identified; when a number of interrelated items requires better definition; when data cannot be easily, quickly, or inexpensively acquired to identify root causes; or when scarce resources demand a carefully focused effort.

There are two approaches to using an interrelationship digraph. The original approach, referred to as the arrow method (see Figure 50), was developed in Japan and uses a series of arrows to graphically portray the directions of known or existing interrelationships. This method works quite nicely for a relatively small group of data elements (see Figure 51).

As the number of elements begins to grow, however, the mass of arrowheads tend to overlap, which causes a confusing picture not unlike a plate of spaghetti.

The GOAL/QPC organization teaches an alternate approach referred to as the *matrix method* (see Figure 52). This approach was especially created to deal with those situations that involve a medium to large number of data elements. The matrix method employs an L-shaped matrix that methodically organizes the multitude of interrelationships among the elements.

Both approaches are designed to facilitate the subsequent analysis to prioritize the elements, that is, to determine the critical/ vital few that have the greatest impact on achieving whatever results are desired.

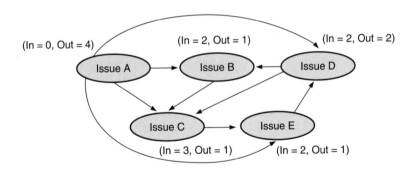

Figure 50   Arrow method.

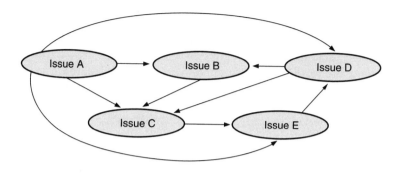

Figure 51   Draw directional.

Issues	A	B	C	D	E	In	Out	Priority
A		↑	↑	↑	↑	0	4	1
B	←		↑	←		2	1	3
C	←	←		←	↑	3	1	3
D	←	↑	↑		←	2	2	2
E	←		←	↑		2	1	3

Figure 52   Matrix method.

ISO 9000:2000

ISO is the acronym used by the International Organization for Standardization to refer to itself. ISO is the short form of the Greek word *isos* meaning *equal*. As of January 2003, ISO had an international membership of 146 national standards bodies and 2,937 technical bodies. Located in Geneva, Switzerland, ISO has about 500 employees in its Central Secretariat.

ISO is chartered to develop and administer, but not to write, more than 13,700 standards including ISO 9000:2000 (the most recent quality management standard). Other standards cover numerous other topics of concern around the globe; ISO 14000:1996 the environmental management standard; ISO 13485:1996 the quality systems for medical devices standard; ISO 16949:2002 the standard for automotive production and relevant service parts organizations; ISO 02859-1:1999, -2:1985, and -4:2002 all standards for sampling procedures for inspection by attributes; and ISO 35342-2:1993 (the standard for statistics vocabulary and symbols for statistical quality control). These standards are prepared by volunteer groups of subject matter experts known as technical committees.

It is not within ISO's charter to issue certificates of registration to its standards. This responsibility falls within the purview of a certification body that has been approved by an accreditation body. An accreditation body approves a registrar or certification body to carry out an ISO standard in specific sectors of business. A company is then issued a certificate of registration to a particular ISO standard by a certification body that has been accredited by an accreditation body. In the United States, the accreditation body is The American National Standards Institute–Registrar Accreditation Board National Accreditation Program (ANSI-RAB NAP).

Once a certification body has been has been approved by the ANSI-RAB NAP for one or more ISO standards, it is authorized to assess a company only against those specific standards for which it has been approved. If the company meets the requirements for that standard, the registrar is authorized to issue a certificate to confirm that the company is in conformance with the standard's requirements. In the United States, this process is referred to as *ISO registration*. Although it is common practice to say that a company is *ISO certified* or *ISO registered,* these terms are technically incorrect since ISO does not register or certify companies to the standards it develops and administers.

With respect to ISO 9000, the quality management standard, it was first issued in 1987, revised in 1994, and then revised again in 2000. ISO 9001:2000, the single standard, has replaced the 1994 versions of ISO 9001, ISO 9002, and ISO 9003. Those companies that were registered to ISO 9000:1994 and wish to maintain their registration to ISO 9000:2000 should have transitioned their company quality manuals to conform to the most recent version by December 15, 2003. An organization can have its system audited against this standard by a specialized independent body, which then issues a certificate of conformity.

Companies wishing to make the transition from ISO 9000:1994 to ISO 9000:2000, or those that want to gain ISO 9000 registration for the first time, should contact the ANSI-RAB and request a copy of ISO 9004:2000. The latter is a guidance document that provides the entire text of ISO 9000:2000 plus additional guidance for companies wanting to go beyond the basics of the quality management system described in ISO 9000:2000.

J

JUST-IN-TIME (JIT): KANBAN INVENTORY VERSUS JIT TRAINING

The common use of the phrase *just in time* refers to the act of getting something done with no time to spare: at precisely the moment when it must be done or else it's too late. In the world of work, *just in time* (JIT) takes on additional meanings. Sometimes it refers to a form of inventory management, and at other times, it indicates a type of personnel training.

Inventory Management

In the context of inventory management, JIT describes a system of process planning that minimizes the amount of *work in process* (WIP) to the smallest amount possible. WIP is that portion of the inventory being used to produce a product located somewhere between the start and the finish of the production process. Often, the WIP in each of the subprocesses is managed to keep the slowest subprocess fully operating. The slowest subprocess is a constraint commonly known as the *bottleneck process* or simply the *bottleneck*.

In some literature, JIT is described primarily in terms of supplier deliveries. This is a case where supplier deliveries are timed so that a process has just enough material for the smallest interval of time that makes sense for that process. For example, the stocking of raw materials or parts might be closer to economic optimality if it takes place on a daily or weekly basis rather than having each delivery include two weeks' or a month's worth of material.

Just in time can be applied to internal operations as well as supplier transactions. For example, a JIT operation that assembles electronic parts could have all its processes operating on a JIT basis with respect to each other. In this case, a preceding operation would work on a part only when it was time to replace one being worked on in the next operation or step.

JIT is often coupled with some form of simple, visual restocking guide. The guide might be a small rack that is kept filled, or it could be one or two taped part outlines on a workbench. It can also take the form of small cards that signal it is time to minimally restock. This type of visual cue is called a *kanban inventory control system* or *kanban*.

JIT Training

Education helps us to understand *why*. Training helps us to understand *how*. JIT training helps us to learn *how* when we most need the help, that is, just before we must have the information if we are going to be able to do our jobs well. Training received too early is information lost over time for lack of application.

KANO MODEL

Many "experts" insist that customers don't really know what they want, they have to be told. They're wrong, dead wrong! Customers do know what they want, but may not be proficient at describing their needs. By understanding the three types of customer needs and how to reveal them, you'll be well on your way to knowing the customer's needs as well as, or perhaps better than, they do.

The Kano model is quite useful in gaining a thorough understanding of a customer's needs. The resulting *verbatims* should be translated and transformed using the voice of the customer table that, subsequently, becomes an excellent input as the *whats* in a QFD house of quality.

There are two dimensions presented in the Kano model:

- Achievement (the horizontal axis) which runs from the supplier (didn't do it at all) to the supplier (did it very well).

- Satisfaction (the vertical axis) that goes from *total dissatisfaction* with the product or service to *total satisfaction* with the product or service.

Dr. Noriaki Kano isolated and identified three levels of customer expectations: that is, what it takes to positively impact customer satisfaction. As portrayed in Figure 53, there are three levels of need: expected, normal, and exciting.

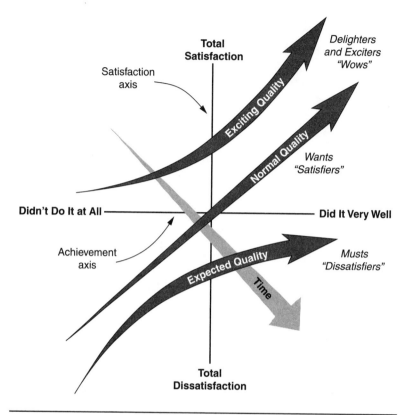

Figure 53   Kano model.

Expected Needs

Fully satisfying the customer at this level simply gets a supplier into the market. The entry level expectations are referred to as the *must* level qualities, properties, or attributes. These expectations are also known as the *dissatisfiers* because by themselves they are unable to fully satisfy a customer; however, failure to provide these basic expectations will cause dissatisfaction. Examples include: attributes relative to safety, latest generation automotive components such as a self-starter, and the use of all new parts if a product is offered for sale as previously unused or new. The *musts* include customer assumptions, expected qualities, expected functions, and other *unspoken* expectations.

Figure 54   Types of customer requirements.

Normal Needs

These are the qualities, attributes, and characteristics that keep a supplier in the market. These next higher level expectations are known as the *wants* or the *satisfiers* because they are the ones that customers will specify as though from a list. They can either satisfy or dissatisfy the customer depending on their presence or absence. The *wants* include *voice of the customer* requirements and other *spoken* expectations (see Figure 54).

Exciting Needs

These are features and properties that make a supplier a leader in the market. The highest level of customer expectations, as described by Kano, is termed the *wow* level qualities, properties, or attributes. These expectations are also known as the *delighters* or *exciters* because they go well beyond anything the customer might imagine and ask for. Their absence does nothing to hurt a possible sale, but their presence improves the likelihood of purchase. *Wows* not only excite customers to make on-the-spot purchases but make them return for future purchases. These are *unspoken* ways of knocking the customer's socks off. Examples include: heads-up display in a front windshield, forward- and rear-facing radars, and a 100,000 mile warranty.

Over time, as demonstrated by the arrow going from top left to bottom right in the Kano model, *wows* become *wants* become *musts*, for example, automobile self-starters and automatic transmissions. The organization that gets ahead and stays ahead is constantly pulsing its customers to identify the next *wows*. The best *wows*, plenty of *wants*, and all the *musts* are what it takes to become and remain an industry leader.

Figure 54 further clarifies the various types of customer requirements with respect to home buyers.

L

LEADERSHIP VERSUS MANAGEMENT

In his 1990 text *Why Leaders Can't Lead*, Warren Bennis noted that, "Leaders are people who do the right thing; managers are people who do things right . . ." Are you a leader, a manager, or both? Before you respond, look at the attributes of a leader versus those of a manager.

First, what expectations are associated with managing? The key function of a manager is to get results. To obtain sustained results, a manager must plan, direct, control, supervise, organize, coordinate, and strategize.

Leading, on the other hand, is associated with an entirely different set of expectations. The major responsibility of a leader is to improve systems. To improve systems, a leader must share an organizational vision, empower the workforce, align organizational resources, coach individuals, enable the workforce, and care for people.

Management is what people do to *run* an organization. This has daily implications as well as long-term expectations and varies according to the level of organization within which a manager resides. While senior level managers concern themselves with long-term activities, first level managers focus their attention on day-to-day operations. In between, middle level managers share their focus on both future and present activities, depending upon their current organizational assignment.

Leadership goes beyond management. Leaders, by virtue of their charisma, as well as their reputations for caring and being "people persons," are able to capture and direct the individual and collective energies and abilities of their employees, associates, and peers. Leaders take on many roles that better enable them to achieve both individual and organizational goals. These roles include coaching, counseling, confronting, mentoring, empowering, and continuing their own as well as others' personal management development, educating, and enabling.

The personal attributes of a leader are as follows:

- Creates more leaders

- Listens

- Focuses on customers

- Continuously improves his or her education

- Knows when to coach and when to judge

- Bases decisions on data

- Removes obstacles to enjoying work

- Provides resources, direction, and understanding

- Understands variation

- Is actively involved

- Works to improve systems and processes

- Builds commitment

- Creates trust

- Inspires confidence

- Forgives mistakes

- Says "thanks"

LEAN ENTERPRISE

A lean enterprise operates profitably with shorter manufacturing runs by building to customer orders rather than marketing forecasts. This results in dramatic reductions in new product development times.

These capabilities, often referred to as *lean manufacturing*, reduce the cycle time to market. The capabilities result from the introduction of more flexible, more automated, computer controlled production machinery. The efficiency and flexibility created by these innovations in manufacturing and assembly processes result in expanded model variety as seen in Figure 55.

The lean enterprise model (LEM) is a systematic framework for organizing and disseminating research results of the Lean Aerospace Initiative. It encompasses lean enterprise principles and practices and is populated by research-based benchmarking data derived from surveys, case studies, and other research activities.

The LEM is designed to assist interested organizations to identify and assess their own leanness and processes. It is intended to help leverage opportunities for organizational change and to support future lean efforts. The LEM is composed of five principles, four enterprise-level metrics, and 12 overarching practices.

LIST REDUCTION

List reduction is a technique used by team or group facilitators to assist in reducing a large number of ideas to a much smaller, more manageable list, usually three to five items. It is a structured series or rounds of voting designed to assist cross-functional teams of subject matter experts in dealing with an otherwise unmanageable list of topics. Alternatively, list reduction can be effectively used to assign operational priorities to each item in a list of many items.

Whether the team is small (three to five persons) or large (more than 10 persons), this technique is ideally suited to bring closure to discussions regarding which topics are most or least important. As in any situation when a facilitator is leading the discussion, it is strongly recommended that a disinterested, unbiased third party be used to keep the team or group on track.

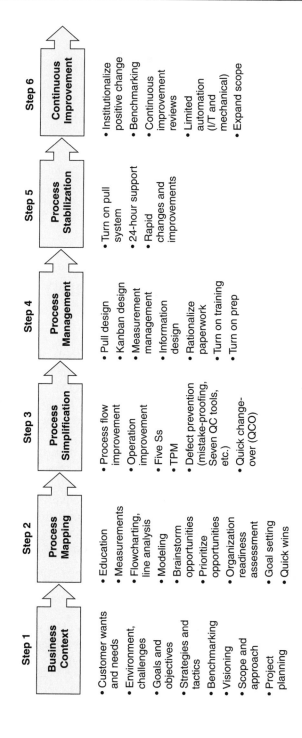

Step 1

Business Context

- Customer wants and needs
- Environment, challenges
- Goals and objectives
- Strategies and tactics
- Benchmarking
- Visioning
- Scope and approach
- Project planning

Step 2

Process Mapping

- Education
- Measurements
- Flowcharting, line analysis
- Modeling
- Brainstorm opportunities
- Prioritize opportunities
- Organization readiness assessment
- Goal setting
- Quick wins

Step 3

Process Simplification

- Process flow improvement
- Operation improvement
- Five Ss
- TPM
- Defect prevention (mistake-proofing, Seven QC tools, etc.)
- Quick change-over (QCO)

Step 4

Process Management

- Pull design
- Kanban design
- Measurement management
- Information design
- Rationalize paperwork
- Turn on training
- Turn on prep

Step 5

Process Stabilization

- Turn on pull system
- 24-hour support
- Rapid changes and improvements

Step 6

Continuous Improvement

- Institutionalize positive change
- Benchmarking
- Continuous improvement reviews
- Limited automation (I/T and mechanical)
- Expand scope

Figure 55   Lean enterprise process flowchart.

MATRIX-BASED MANAGEMENT

Introduction

The seven management and planning (7-MP) tools were introduced and described by Mizuno in his text *The Seven New QC Tools* in 1981. Seven years later, Michael Brassard of GOAL/QPC wrote the first American text on this topic, *The Memory Jogger Plus*. Both of these books, as well as several others written since then, describe the 7-MP tools.

The 7-MP tools include affinity analysis, interrelationship digraph, matrix analysis, prioritization matrix, tree diagram, process decision program chart, and arrow network diagram. Each of these tools provides an important analytical capability to effectively deal with nonquantitative data, that is, qualitative or communications data.

One of the most frequently used of the 7-MP tools is the matrix. A broad variety of matrices is available for everyday use to facilitate many of management's most basic challenges.

Matrix Definitions

matrix—A rectangular arrangement of numbers and/or symbols
    designed to present and analyze various types of data in
    a visual format that provides greater understanding than a
    table of data.

management—Selection and allocation of material and financial resources needed to accomplish specific tasks, projects, and assignments as well as selection, training, and assignment of personnel resources needed for the same purposes.

matrix-based management—Fulfillment of some or all of one's managerial responsibilities through the use of one or more matrices to determine the most logical allocation of all available resources.

Types of Matrices

L-Shaped: X versus Y

This matrix format accommodates two variables, X and Y, in juxtaposition with the intent of making comparisons or demonstrating relationships between the two variables. An L-shaped matrix is presented in Figure 56.

T-Shaped: X versus Y and X versus Z

This matrix is designed to handle three variables, X, Y, and Z, using two separate and distinct L-shaped matrices that have been joined at a common axis. The formation and result of this joining process is presented in Figure 57.

Y-Shaped: X versus Y, X versus Z, and Y versus Z

This matrix is also designed to handle three variables, X, Y, and Z. The formation of the Y-shaped matrix begins with a T-shaped matrix and proceeds to bend the arms of the T to form a Y. The formation and result of this bending process is presented in Figure 58.

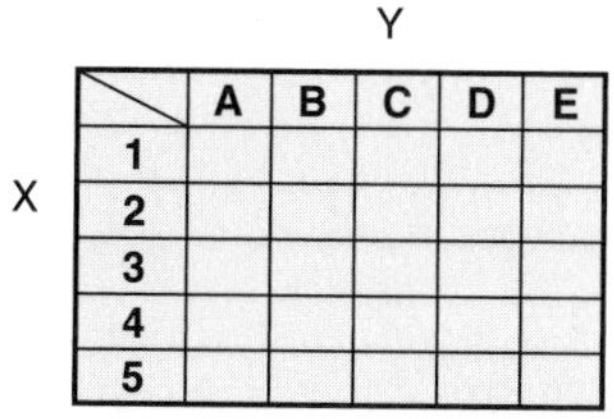

Figure 56   L-shaped matrix.

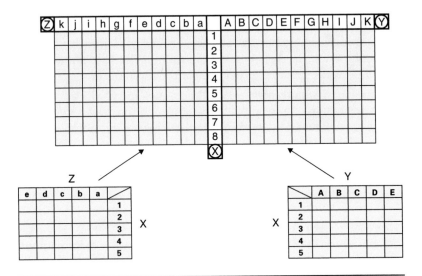

Figure 57   T-shaped matrix.

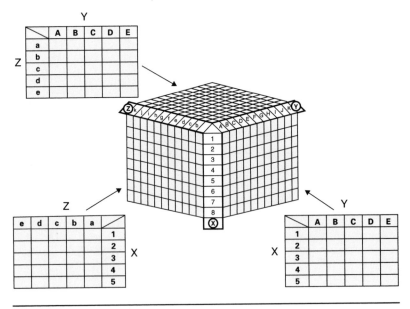

Figure 58   Y-shaped matrix.

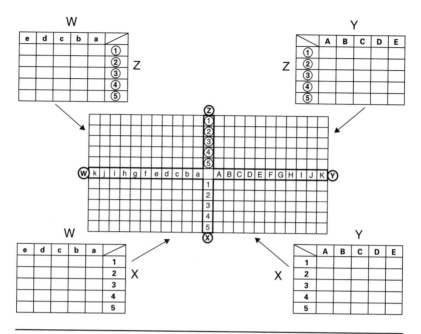

Figure 59 X-shaped matrix.

X-Shaped: X versus Y, X versus W, Z versus Y, and Z versus W

This matrix is designed to handle four variables, *W*, *X*, *Y*, and *Z*, using four separate and distinct L-shaped matrices that have been joined at their four common axes. The formation and result of this joining process is presented in Figure 59.

C-Shaped: X versus Y versus Z

This matrix is designed to handle three variables, *X*, *Y*, and *Z*, using three separate and distinct L-shaped matrices that have been joined at their three common axes. This is the only one of the matrices discussed that possesses the capability to present data in a three-dimensional format, that is, a point in space whose location is dependent upon the magnitude of all three variables. The formation and result of this joining process is presented in Figure 60.

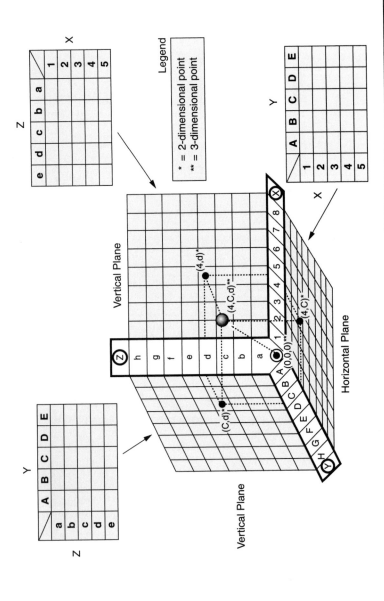

Figure 60 C-shaped matrix.

Example Applications

To facilitate the total understanding of the five matrices, several example applications have been developed (see Figure 61). Four variables are introduced for each of four separate scenarios, but not every variable is employed in every matrix.

The first scenario focuses on manufacturing, the second on services, the third on a division of the federal government, and the fourth on education. The scenarios and variables are presented as follows:

Using the template provided, sketch an L-shaped matrix for the manufacturing scenario based on variables X and Y. Try it two more times, first using X and Z and then using Y and Z.

Now join the first two L-shaped matrices at their common X axis to create a T-shaped matrix. At this point, you have the capability to simultaneously compare various values of X with values of Y on one side of the T-shaped matrix and with values of Z on the other side.

Bend the arms of the T-shaped matrix upward to form a Y-shaped matrix. You still have the capability to conduct the X versus Y and X versus Z analyses just completed, but now with the added capability to simultaneous perform Y versus Z analyses. Thus, in a single glance, you can understand three separate but related relationships and are better equipped to make more informed decisions.

You can expand your analysis capability by using the X-shaped matrix. From the previous analyses using the original T-shaped matrix, you know what the X versus Y and X versus Z relationships look like. Now, form a second T-shaped matrix containing the W versus Y and W versus Z relationships. Then bring the two T-shaped matrices together at their common axes, Y and Z. Although you cannot

Variables	Manufacturing	Services	Government (IRS)	Education
W	Accidents reported	Complaints received	Errors detected	Student challenges
X	Time units, week number	Time units, day number	Time units, month number	Time units, semester number
Y	Items produced	Services provided	Tax returns received	Tests administered
Z	Defects detected	Errors identified	Tax returns audited	Mistakes detected

Figure 61 Scenarios and variables.

evaluate the *Y* versus *Z* relationship as you can with the Y-shaped matrix, you can simultaneously study all four bivariate relationships: *X* versus *Y*, *X* versus *Z*, *W* versus *Y*, and *W* versus *Z*. Give this a try before moving on to the final matrix.

Using the C-shaped matrix, analyze one of the comparisons already studied, *X* versus *Y*. Since you will be working in three dimensions, use the X-shaped matrix of *X* versus *Y* as the base and place the Z-axis in the vertical position. This results in three L-shaped matrices, each of which is perpendicular to the other two: *X* versus *Y*, *X* versus *Z*, and *Y* versus *Z*. The resultant construct appears as a room corner with the floor as the *X* versus *Y* plane, and the two intersecting walls as the *X* versus *Z* and *Y* versus *Z* planes. With knowledge of specific values for *X*, *Y*, and *Z*, you can determine the spatial location of this point and any other point in relationship to each other.

Further Applications

It is appropriate to provide some additional examples to emphasize the broad scope of applications to which matrices have already been put. There's hardly a place in industry, services, government, or education where matrices have not already been applied. But be assured that this is just the beginning; there is a long way to travel before every opportunity to acquire additional understanding through the use of the various matrices have reached their full potential:

- *Manufacturing.* Assignment of orders or jobs to specific machines

- *Equipment/location/personnel.* Selection based on rank ordering of weighted criteria to prioritize available choices

- *Strategic planning.* Assignment of personnel and/or organizational functions to responsibility for strategic/long-term goals as well as tactical/short-term goals

- *Transportation.* Selection of routes to be used based on tradeoffs between cost, time, available equipment, and trained personnel

- *Purchasing.* Selection of vendors or goods based on rank-ordering of weighted criteria to prioritize available choices

Conclusion

This has been an attempt to bring together a variety of related ideas. If you have some example applications using any of the matrices that you believe would be of interest to others, write to the author, so they can be considered for inclusion in a subsequent edition of this book.

MEASURES OF CENTRAL TENDENCY

The three most widely used measures of central tendency are the *mean* (arithmetic mean or average), the *median* (center point), and the *mode* (value that occurs most frequently). Each measure has its own symbol or notation (see Table 2).

A common data pool will help to better understand how to determine each measure of central tendency. Our data pool has five values ($n = 5$): 7, 3, 5, 1, and 9.

Mean

Sum all the values (data points) in the data pool and divide the sum by the number of values (the sample size n).

$$\bar{x} = \frac{7+3+5+1+9}{5} = \frac{25}{5} = 5$$

Median

Arrange the values in the data pool into an array of numbers from the largest value to the smallest or vice versa. The center point is the median. It has as many numbers above it as it does below. This is true with an *odd* number of values in the data pool.

Table 2 Measures of central tendency notation.

Name	Notation
Mean	$\bar{x}$ (x-bar for a single sample)
	$\bar{\bar{x}}$ (x–double bar for a sampling distribution)
	μ (the Greek letter *mu* for a population)
Median	Md
Mode	Mo

If there is an *even* number of values in the data pool, identify the two values in the middle of the array and calculate their average value. This average of the two centermost values is the median:

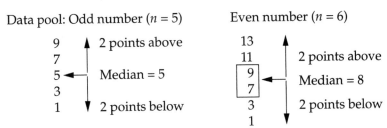

Data pool: Odd number ($n = 5$)   Even number ($n = 6$)

Mode

Arrange the values in the data pool into an array of numbers from the largest value to the smallest or vice versa. The value that occurs most frequently is the mode (unimodal or one mode). If two values occur most frequently, the data pool is bimodal.

Data pool: A ($n = 6$)   B ($n = 6$)

```
    13              13
    11              11
    11  Mode = 11   11  Mode #1 = 11
     9               9
     7               9  Mode #2 = 9
     3               7
```

Unimodal   *Bimodal*

MEASURES OF DISPERSION

The six most widely used measures of dispersion are the *range*, the *average deviation*, the *standard deviation*, the *quartile*, the *decile*, and the *percentile*. Data dispersion results from inconsistent, unpredictable performance. A predictable process produces results that are consistent from one time period to the next. An unpredictable process produces results that are widely dispersed.

Range

Identify the largest and the smallest values in a data pool. The range is the absolute difference (without regard to the mathematical sign) between these two values. It is standard practice to subtract the smallest value from the largest value. As a result, the range is always either zero (if the two numbers are the same) or positive.

Data pool ($n = 5$)

7
3
5
1 ← Smallest value
9 ← Largest value

$$\text{Range} = x_{\text{Largest}} - x_{\text{Smallest}}$$
$$= 9 - 1$$
$$= 8$$

Average Deviation

The average deviation is calculated using the formula

$$AD = \frac{\Sigma |x_i - \bar{x}|}{n}$$

The notation " | " indicates the absolute value of the difference without regard to the mathematical sign.

Data pool $(n = 5)$ \qquad Since $\bar{x} = 5$

x	$|x_i - \bar{x}|$
7	$7 - 5 = 2$
3	$3 - 5 = 2$
5	$5 - 5 = 0$
1	$1 - 5 = 4$
9	$9 - 5 = 4$
	$\Sigma |xi - x| = 12$

$$AD = \frac{\Sigma |x_i - \bar{x}|}{n} = \frac{12}{5} = 2.40$$

Standard Deviation

The sample standard deviation is calculated using the formula

$$SSD = \sqrt{\frac{\Sigma (x - \bar{x})^2}{n - 1}}$$

In this example, the data pool has five values ($n = 5$); they are, in no particular order: 7, 3, 5, 1, and 9. From the formula, you will need to know their average, $\bar{x}$.

$$\bar{x} = \frac{7+3+5+1+9}{5}$$

$$= \frac{25}{5}$$

$$= 5$$

You can also see from the formula that you will need to know the value of the term $(x - \bar{x})$ for each value of x.

x	$(x - \bar{x})$
7	$7 - 5 = 2$
3	$3 - 5 = -2$
5	$5 - 5 = 0$
1	$1 - 5 = -4$
9	$9 - 5 = 4$

Furthermore, you will need to know the sum of all these $(x - \bar{x})$ terms.

x	$(x - \bar{x})$	$(x - \bar{x})^2$
7	2	4
3	-2	4
5	0	0
1	-4	16
9	4	16
		$\Sigma(x - \bar{x})^2 = 40$

Next, divide $\Sigma (x - \bar{x})^2$ by $n - 1$. In this example, n is the size of our data pool, that is, $n = 5$.

$$n - 1 = 5 - 1 = 4$$

Since we have finished our calculations under the square root sign, the calculation of the sample standard deviation can be completed.

$$SSD = \sqrt{\frac{40}{4}}$$
$$= \sqrt{10}$$
$$= 3.16$$

Quartiles

A quartile is 25 percent of whatever is being evaluated. There are four quartiles used to describe a data pool. The first (top) quartile and the fourth (bottom) quartile represent the top 25 percent of all the values and the bottom 25 percent, respectively. The second and third quartiles are immediately above and below the median.

Data Pool (n = 20)

	Quartile			
	1st	**2nd**	**3rd**	**4th**
	50	44	38	34
	49	43	38	33
	47	42	37	32
	45	41	36	31
	45	40	35	30
		Median = 39		

Deciles

A decile is 10 percent of whatever is being evaluated. There are 10 deciles used to describe a data pool.

Data Pool (n = 20)

	Decile									
1st	**2nd**	**3rd**	**4th**	**5th**	**6th**	**7th**	**8th**	**9th**	**10th**
50	47	45	43	41	38	37	35	33	31
49	45	44	42	40	38	36	34	32	30
				Median = 39					

Percentiles

A percentile is one percent of whatever is being evaluated. There are 100 percentiles used to describe a data pool. Thirty percentiles are 30 percent of whatever is being observed, for example, 30 percent of $n = 20$ units is (30% or 0.30) times (20) = (0.30)(20) = 6 units.

MIND MAPPING

The key to breaking old paradigms is to use the intuitive powers of the mind. Mind mapping is a powerful technique for invoking the creative part of the brain. It works with colors and images to promote the visualization of ideas rather than evaluation via logic. (see Figure 62)

It is a tool for organizing a large number of ideas and, as such, should be considered for use with affinity analysis, one of the seven management and planning tools. In addition, mind mapping has been successfully used before the start of a brainstorming session.

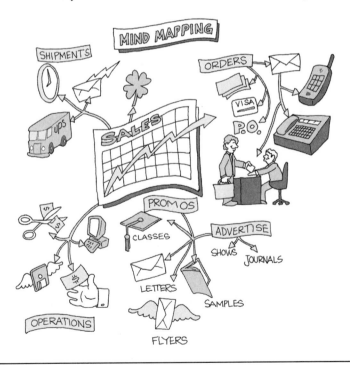

Figure 62 Mind mapping.

It is usually performed by a small group working in silence around a common map. In larger groups, it is recommended that one person be the recorder to draw the map while the others provide the images.

Mind mapping begins when the participating group or team clearly defines a specific topic. A symbol of the topic, referred to as the central image, is drawn in the center of a piece of paper. For the sake of clarity, a word or two may be placed next to the symbol.

Then, either in silence or with a background of relaxing music, the members of the group concentrate on the topic. As ideas or images come to mind, they are recorded around the central image. Colors and symbols are used to stimulate the creativity of the team members. One word may be added for clarity.

This is followed by using a line to connect each image to the central image. At this point, the team members focus on each new image and capture the additional images it stimulates. This process continues until the team runs out of ideas.

Finally, ideas with common themes are grouped by drawing a colored line around them, marking them with a common code, or redrawing the map to cluster them together.

Taking frequent advantage of mind mapping will improve a team's ability to involve the creative right brains of the team's members in decision making.

MORPHOLOGICAL BOX

The morphological box is designed to assist a team in the identification of all the practical solutions to a problem. This objective is accomplished by first defining the boundaries of all the possible solutions, that is, the solution space. Then the team selects parameters and options within the parameters.

The parameters are identified or discovered by asking simple questions, such as: "What are the attributes or characteristics which are important to us when we make a final decision?" The options are determined by asking other simple questions: "For each parameter, what are all the acceptable choices available to us?" The multitude of options available for selection within each parameter produces an extensive variety of unique combinations or scenarios from which the team selects the optimal solution.

Compared to brainstorming, the morphological box is quite suitable for use in a broad variety of applications. The box possesses the additional advantage of superiority in dealing with highly complex problems. This advantage results from the box's capacity for its solution parameters to be adjusted to virtually any level of complexity.

Effective application of the morphological box requires that team members have analytical abilities, sharp thinking, and the power to precisely define a problem and its components. For a participant to be successful in dealing with a problem when using a morphological box, he or she should possess an extensive knowledge about the specific technology or field in question.

During a brainstorming session, a team member can make relevant contributions without being a subject matter expert (SME) since the contributions made by other team members could stimulate an unusual idea. However, this level of knowledge is not enough to create a useful morphological box. This requirement for more thorough knowledge indicates that the box is an excellent tool for application by a team of SMEs.

When a morphological box is applied to complex situations or problems, the extent of the problem-solving work required exceeds that demanded in a conventional creativity session. It would be overly ambitious to attempt to clarify any final results without working to achieve the team's objective for more than just a couple of days. For these and other related reasons, the box should be used when a team must address highly complex or extremely significant problems.

Figure 63 demonstrates how a screenwriter might determine the parameters of his or her next screenplay. In this simple example, only five parameters are considered down the left side of the morphological box. Then one option is selected from each of the five options available for each parameter. One of the 25 choices from which the author could select is noted as part of this example.

Genre = Mystery   Male lead = 40s
Locale = New York   Female lead = 50s   Time period = 1920s

Parameters	Options				
Genre	Mystery	Musical	Sci Fi	Action	Teen
Locale	San Diego	New York	Phoenix	Dallas	Boston
Male lead	60s	50s	40s	30s	20s
Female lead	60s	50s	40s	30s	20s
Time period	1920s	1940s	1960s	1980s	2000s

Figure 63   Movie screenplay development.

MUDA (WASTE)

Muda is a Japanese term meaning *waste,* specifically any human activity that absorbs resources but does not create value. The following are included within this concept: human error which requires corrective action, production of items no one will purchase (thus forcing the accumulation of both inventories and returned goods), steps within a process that provide no value-added content, transport of employees and goods from one point to another without rationale or reason, groups of employees positioned in a downstream activity who are standing around waiting for work because an upstream activity has failed to deliver on time, goods and services that don't meet the needs of the customer.

Muda is the source of the hidden factory. Said in reverse, to eliminate or at least substantially reduce the hidden factory, the vital or critical few muda must be isolated through the sequential application of the 7-QC tools such as Pareto analysis and cause-and-effect analysis.

MULTIVOTING

Multivoting is a quick and easy way for a group or team to determine the highest priority items within a list of items. It is best suited for large groups and long lists. Its simplicity helps a team:

- Prioritize a large list without creating a win–lose situation in the group or team that generated the list.

- Separate the vital or critical few items from the trivial many on a large list. This concept was originated as a part of Pareto analysis, one of the seven quality control (7-QC) tools.

Multivoting begins with each team member receiving the right to vote up to X times, where X is approximately equal to one-third to one-half the number of items on a list. Then the members vote individually for the items they believe have the highest priority or the greatest importance.

At this point, the team leader or facilitator compiles the total votes given to each item. A tally sheet, one of the 7-QC tools, is well-suited to this task. The team then selects the leading four to six items for discussion and prioritization relative to each other. When the top four to six items can't be established, those having the fewest votes are removed from the list, and another vote is conducted.

Members of a system program office attended many meetings at different locations around the country. The meetings were not always as productive as they might have been, so the division chiefs called a meeting in hope of improving the situation. A brainstorming session produced the following list:

1. No agenda
2. No clear objective
3. Going off on tangents
4. Extraneous topics
5. Unproductive
6. Time spent on travel
7. Money spent on travel
8. Too much "dog and pony"
9. Problems not mentioned
10. Unclear charts
11. Few meaningful metrics
12. Trouble calling home office
13. No parking
14. No administrative support

To reduce this list to a manageable size, each group member was given seven votes (half of the 14 items). As a result of the vote, the group chose to focus on problems 2, 6, 7, 8, 10, and 11.

/	1. No agenda
////	2. No clear objective
//	3. Going off on tangents
/	4. Extraneous topics
//	5. Unproductive
ЖＬ	6. Time spent on travel
ЖＬ	7. Money spent on travel
ЖＬ	8. Too much "dog and pony"

//   9. Problems not mentioned

〦〦〦 / 10. Unclear charts

//// 11. Few meaningful metrics

//   12. Trouble calling home office

0   13. No parking

/   14. No administrative support

NOMINAL GROUP TECHNIQUE (NGT)

The nominal group technique (NGT) is a variation on brainstorming. Its purpose is the same, but the methodology is somewhat different. It can help in group problem solving when there is subtle pressure toward conformity. ("If you don't agree with the group, you're not acting like a member of the team.")

It can also counter status effects; for example, senior or more experienced members of a team are assumed to be more knowledgeable, thus making other members reluctant to participate or bring up completely different ideas. It's also easy for groups to go off on tangents, getting too caught up with one idea or train of thought; members are sometimes unwilling to say something that sounds completely off the wall compared to what other team members are discussing. Likewise, a group can be too narrowly focused.

NGT begins with all the team members writing down their ideas on paper without any discussion. After everyone has generated a list, the facilitator uses a round-robin method of listing each person's ideas on flip charts, taking one idea from each person in succession until all ideas have been listed.

There is still no discussion during this phase. Only after all the ideas have been written down and posted around the room does the group begin discussion, asking for clarification of each idea. The person who listed the idea should respond to any questions about the idea, but others are permitted to join in. Sometimes,

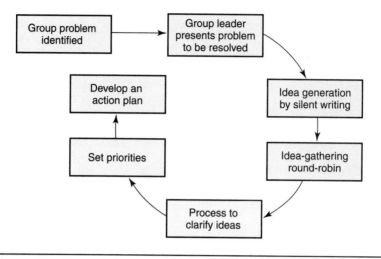

Figure 64 Steps of the nominal group technique.

ideas can be combined if the group agrees that they are essentially the same.

The next phase of the nominal group technique is to narrow the list down to a manageable number by prioritizing each idea. There are several ways to accomplish this, and one of the best is multivoting (see page 113). Once the list of items has been prioritized, the group can begin to develop an action plan for continuous improvement (see Figure 64).

Nominal Group Technique Example

The following office problems were identified in a brainstorming session:

A. Ineffective organizational structure

B. Poor communications outside the office

C. Lack of training

D. Poor communications within the office

E. Unclear mission and objectives

F. Poor distribution of office mail

G. Lack of feedback on reports on management

Each group member then wrote the letters *A* through *G* on a piece of paper and prioritized each problem from 1 to 7 (lowest to highest), using each number only once. The results were summarized as follows:

Problem	Person 1	2	3	4	5	Total	Priority	
A	6	5	7	5	6	29	#2	
B	3	2	4	1	3	13	#5	
C	1	1	2	2	2	8	#7	Lowest priority
D	4	4	5	6	4	23	#4	
E	7	7	6	7	5	32	#1	Highest priority
F	2	3	1	3	1	10	#6	
G	5	6	3	4	7	25	#3	

ORTHOGONAL ARRAY

An orthogonal array is a technique that is important for organizations using or planning to use robust design or DOE.

In the course of designing a simple experiment, suppose a team has three factors that need to be studied at two levels each. Using the common practice of factorial design, the number of experimental runs needed for a full factorial design is equal to the number of factor levels (in this case = 2) raised to the power of the number of factors (in this case = 3). Two raised to the third power or $2^3 = 8$ experimental runs. The layout of the eight runs is as follows:

Run	Factors		
	A	B	C
1	1	1	1
2	1	2	1
3	1	1	2
4	1	2	2
5	2	1	1
6	2	2	1
7	2	1	2
8	2	2	2

The 1s and 2s in the factor columns are factor levels. Thus, in Run 1, Factors A, B, and C are all at level 1; in Run 4, Factor A is at level 1, but Factors *B* and *C* are at level 2. In Run 7, Factor *B* is at level 1, but Factors *A* and *C* are at level 2.

A full factorial design is used when an experimenter needs to study both main effects (the results of just the factors) and interaction effects (the results of combining two or more factors). When an experimenter needs to study only the main effects or a combination of the main effects and only some of the interactions, then a full factorial design is not required and a fractional factorial design can be selected.

In the preceding three factor–two level example, any four runs would constitute a one-half fractional factorial (Runs 1, 2, 3, and 4; 3, 4, 5, and 6; or 1, 4, 6, and 7). These are all one-half fractional factorials because they have half as many runs as the full factorial from which they were drawn. In the third set of runs, there is a fractional factorial with some special properties, and so this design is referred to as an *orthogonal array*. When this set is studied, it appears as follows:

	Factors		
Run	**A**	**B**	**C**
1	1	1	1
4	1	2	2
6	2	1	2
7	2	2	1

Special property 1: An equal number of 1s and 2s must exist in each column. This balance is one of the three properties that must be present for a fractional factorial to qualify as an orthogonal array.

	Factors		
Run	**A**	**B**	**C**
1	1	1	1
4	1	2	2

Special property 2: Looking at any factor for those runs where the levels are the same (Runs 1 and 4 when Factor *A* is at level 1), then the frequency of occurrence of the levels of the other factors must be equal (in this case, levels 1 and 2 for Factors *B* and *C*). There is a single *1* and a single *2* in the remaining columns (Factors *B* and *C*).

Special property 3: To qualify as an orthogonal array, a fractional factorial must be the smallest design (the one with the least number of runs) for a given combination of factors and factor levels, and it must possess the first two special properties.

These orthogonal arrays are important for use by experimenters because they permit studies to be conducted without having to pay for more runs than are actually necessary. In the example, if there were no need to study the three two-way interactions ($A \times B$, $A \times C$, and $B \times C$) or the three-way interaction ($A \times B \times C$), it wouldn't make sense to use a full factorial when a one-half fractional factorial can provide all the needed information.

In this case, the orthogonal array design costs half as much and takes half as long to conduct because only half the runs are necessary. In cases where an experimenter is studying more factors and factor levels than in this example, it is quite common to use an orthogonal array that is a small fraction of its corresponding full factorial. Clearly a major savings in cost and time can be realized.

There is still another important advantage in using an orthogonal array. When a design of experiments is performed using an orthogonal array, the results of the experiment can identify a combination of factors and factor levels that yield the best results (in terms of whatever performance measures/metrics are used) even if that combination was not one that was contained in the original orthogonal array.

For example, in the foregoing case, the DOE might identify Factors A, B, and C all at level 2 as the optimal design combination even though that combination was not part of the experiment. Recall that it was a part of the original full factorial, but not a part of the subsequent fractional factorial (orthogonal array). When this occurs, a confirmation run is necessary using the optimal design combination.

PAIRWISE RANKING

Pairwise ranking is a structured method for ranking a small list of items in priority order. It can help a team prioritize a small list as well as make decisions by consensus.

To begin a pairwise ranking, a pairwise matrix is constructed. Each box in the matrix represents the intersection (or pairing) of two items. When the list has five items, the pairwise matrix will look like Figure 65, with the top box representing idea 1 paired with idea 2:

The team begins the process by using consensus to determine which of two ideas is preferred for each pairing. Then for each pair, the number of the preferable idea is written in the appropriate box. This process is repeated until the matrix is completed (see Figure 66).

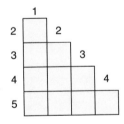

Figure 65 A pairwise matrix.

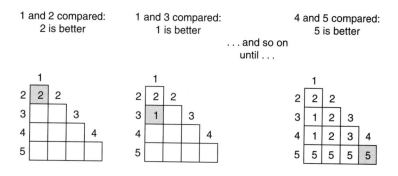

Figure 66 Sequential comparisons leading to a complete pairwise matrix.

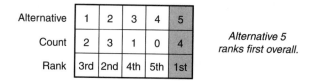

Figure 67 Counts of alternatives.

Alternative	1	2	3	4	5
Count	2	3	1	0	4
Rank	3rd	2nd	4th	5th	1st

Alternative 5 ranks first overall.

Figure 68 Ranking of alternatives.

At this point, the team counts the number of times each alternative appears in the matrix (see Figure 67).

Finally, the alternatives are ranked according to the total number of times they appear in the matrix. To break a tie, where two ideas appear the same number of times, the box in which those two ideas are compared is examined. The idea appearing in that box receives the higher ranking (see Figure 68).

PARETO ANALYSIS

A Pareto diagram is a special form of bar chart used by cross-functional teams to identify and prioritize areas of concern, particularly any change from the status quo. This change could be either a leading process-related problem, such as a particular type of defect or complaint, or it could be an unexplained improvement in a product lot or a process output. A Pareto analysis directs a team's attention to the most frequently occurring or most costly area of concern.

There are three uses and types of Pareto analysis. The *basic* Pareto diagram identifies the *critical few* causes that account for most of the occurrences of the effect under study (see Figure 69). The *comparative* Pareto diagram is time-oriented and focuses on the status of a system, process, or situation on a before-and-after basis, that is, what changes have taken place as a result of an intervention or corrective action (see Figure 70). The *weighted* Pareto diagram provides a measure of significance to factors that may not at first appear to be significant, for example, cost, time, and criticality.

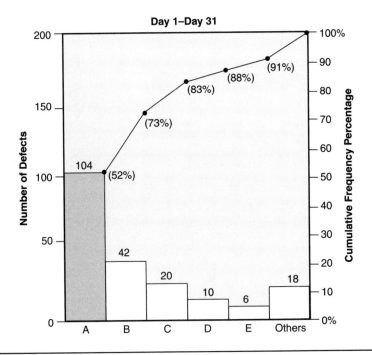

Figure 69   Basic Pareto diagram of nonconforming items.

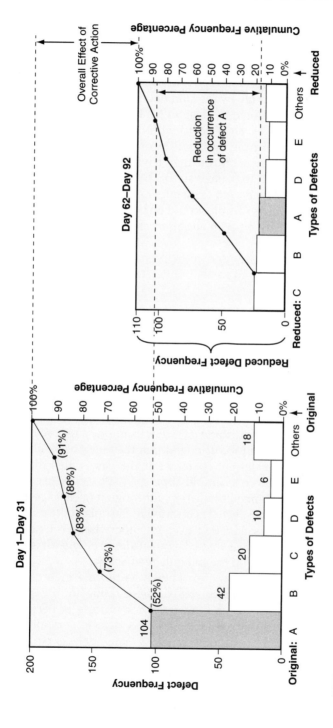

Figure 70 Comparison of Pareto diagrams before and after improvements.

For those who care about such things, Vilfredo Pareto was an economist who lived in the late 19th and early 20th centuries. His writings on European economics included a description of *maldistribution of wealth* within European societies of the time. According to Pareto, this was caused primarily by the land holdings of the aristocracy.

In his early writings, Dr. Joseph M. Juran included a description of the *Pareto Principle*. According to Juran, the greatest payoff comes from focusing on the "critical or vital few" and by temporarily setting aside work on the "trivial many." He advocated use of Pareto analysis to make it simple to select the most important areas of concern. The Pareto Principle is often succinctly described as the 80–20 rule. An example would be that 80 percent of the problems associated with a given situation are the result of 20 percent of its problem sources.

Pareto diagrams are used to help analyze attribute data while histograms are employed to help understand variable data.

PERFORMANCE MEASURES/METRICS: ATTRIBUTE VERSUS VARIABLE DATA

Basically, there are two types of data to collect as a part of a problem-solving process: attribute data and variable data.

Because the level of sensitivity of a measurement depends on the precision of the measuring device, there are times when variable data can be treated as attribute data. For example, suppose that aluminum pins are being produced and that they may be smaller than 1.065 inches in diameter but not larger. In this case, rather than measuring each pin or even a sample of pins, a plate can be used which has a 1.065 inches diameter hole bored through it (a *go/no-go* gauge). Then each pin to be inspected is inserted in the hole. If the pin passes through the hole, it is classified as *accept;* otherwise, it is treated as a *reject.* Thus, the variable is treated as an attribute because it is an efficient way to determine if the pin will be effective.

Performance measures, also known as process metrics or key quality indicators, should be ratios. These ratios are the statistics that describe how well or how poorly a process is performing. Sometimes the ratios have labels such as defects per unit (dpu), defects per defective unit, defects per X units, defects per million opportunities (dpmo), or parts per million (ppm) defect rate (dpmo and ppm are different names for the same ratio). However, there are ratios that do not have labels, for example, C_P (the process capability index) and C_{PK} (the mean-sensitive process capability index). These ratios are covered in detail elsewhere in this book.

PERFORMANCE MEASURES/METRICS: SELECTION PROCESS AND EXAMPLES

Generally speaking, one of the biggest problems associated with continuous improvement and problem solving is the selection of the most appropriate performance measures or performance metrics. Let's use the sport of baseball as an example. A broad variety of performance measures or performance metrics can be used to assess the success or failure of individual players as well as their teams. These ratios will vary depending on a player's position. Pitchers are evaluated using their earned run average (ERA), their total number of strikeouts, and the number of home runs hit against them by opposing batters.

ERA is the number of runs scored against a pitcher per nine innings pitched. An ERA of 2.05 indicates that for multiple games a pitcher had 2.05 runs scored against his pitching for each nine innings pitched.

While a pitcher is rated almost exclusively on his defensive skills, a fielder is evaluated on both his offensive and defensive skills. Offensively, a fielder is rated on his hitting skills including batting percentage (BP), runs batted in (RBI), and slugging average (SA).

BP is the number of hits per number of times at bat. A BP of .400 is exceptional, but rarely achieved, while a BP of .300 is good, and a BP of .100 is typical of most pitchers

Defensively, a fielder is ranked according to fielding percentage (FP), his ability to catch and throw a ball without an error. This includes not dropping a batted ball, not throwing the ball to the wrong base, or not making an inaccurate throw to the correct base. FP is the number of fielding opportunities played without an error divided by the total number of opportunities.

In the world of commerce and industry, a multitude of financial performance measures or performance metrics are in widespread use at the organizational or enterprise level. These include ratios such as return on net assets (RONA) and return on investment (ROI). These ratios and other nonfinancial ratios such as market share and name recognition index are dependent variables which numerically describe the level of success or failure of an organization for a specific period of time, for example, the third quarter of 2003.

Independent Variables	Dependent Variables
Customer satisfaction	Market share
On-time delivery Competitive price Consistent quality Uncompromising service Brand name recognition	Customer satisfaction
Robust design	Consistent quality
Statistical quality control Six Sigma and/or ppm Design of experiments Analysis of variance Statistical process control	Robust design
Process inputs (5Ms and an E)	Stastical process control
Conveyer speed Operating temperature Operator skill level Humidity level Measurement capability	Process inputs (5Ms and an E)

Figure 71   Relationships of independent and dependent variables as performance metrics.

But how these levels of success or failure are achieved is of greater importance (see Figure 71). These are described using independent variables such as customer satisfaction indices, defect rates, and supplier capability indices. When these factors reflect well on an organization, their dependent variables are much more likely to reflect overall enterprise success.

These can be treated as dependent variables with an entirely new set of independent variables such as conveyor speeds, temperature settings, spindle speeds, work-in-process (WIP) levels, and other direct measures of the various production processes that constitute the enterprise systems creating products that generate organizational income.

The most difficult question for most people is what performance measures or performance metrics to use for their system, their process, or their particular step or operation within a process.

The easiest way to respond to this question is to rephrase the question so that it reads, "What's important to either the internal or external customer that can be measured or counted?" If this question can't be answered directly, then try, "What's important to the customer that can't be directly measured or counted, but which can be assessed indirectly using one or more proxy measures or counts?"

A sequence of top-down performance measures or performance metrics can demonstrate this approach to continuous improvement.

PIE CHART

Pie charts, like bar charts, have been in use for as long as most of us can remember. A pie chart is one of many forms of graphical displays of data (see Figure 72). Usually, a tally sheet is converted into a data table that is then converted into a pie chart.

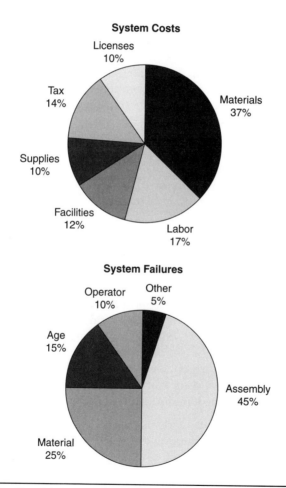

Figure 72 Pie chart examples.

A pie chart helps describe various aspects of the raw data as segments of a pie. The proportion of a pie segment parallels the percentage, item by item, in the corresponding data table. In the event that it is important to emphasize one or more of the major segments of a pie chart, a Pareto chart should be used instead.

PICOS

Description

Dr. J. Ignacio Lopez de Arriortua adopted the Spanish word *picos* (meaning mountain peaks) to identify a process that leads to superiority in three key competitive areas: quality, service, and price. PICOS workshops are *do it now* forms of synchronous workshops. It is a systematic process using a joint customer/supplier team to aggressively identify and eliminate waste and other non-value-added activities.

PICOS workshops can be used both in internal operations and at suppliers. They focus on customer satisfaction by improving quality, service, and cost. The success of the workshops depends upon obtaining management commitment prior to the event, empowerment of the group performing the workshop, a sense of urgency to implement change, measurement of results, and follow-up on longer-term changes that are implemented.

Implementation

General Motors has developed five basic types of PICOS workshops:

1. The *implementation* workshop is the most commonly used. It focuses on a manufacturing process and is used to improve productivity, lead time, floor space utilization, and inventory. The scope is usually limited to a specific area and initial improvements are made during the three-day workshop. Implementation workshop participants must be cross-functional and have knowledge of the process. Continual follow-up and measurement of the identified improvements are crucial to the long-term success of the workshop.

2. *Value management* workshops focus on improving a single product design or manufacturing process by identifying functional value to the customer. Cost savings, implementation cost, and schedule reductions are identified.

3. The *material value chain* workshop involves descending or parallel tiers of suppliers and identifies value-added activities. Improvements are made throughout the supply chain, but primarily in inventory and lead time.

4. The *common enterprise* workshop uses multiple approaches such as implementation, value management, and material value chain workshops. This workshop expands the scope to the total supply chain and involves multiple tiers of suppliers and customers. Measures of success include the four implementation approaches plus design/production cost reduction.

5. The *quality* workshop is usually used in a chronic situation. Measurements are cost of quality, first-time quality, process capability, and overall quality. Elimination of nonconformance is the main focus, with immediate and longer-term changes identified.

POLICY DEPLOYMENT

Policy deployment provides a comprehensive organizational focus that assures management's critical goals will be achieved and empowers employees to self-manage their daily activities. Based on the plan–do–check–act (PDCA) cycle, policy deployment uses an integrated system of forms and rules that encourages employees to analyze situations, create plans for improvement, conduct performance audits, and take appropriate actions.

Policy deployment is referred to by a variety of terms such as hoshin kanri, hoshin planning, hoshin, management by planning, or management by policy. This operating philosophy/management system was first developed in Japan to communicate organizational policy to all employees and to implement the strategic intent of the entire enterprise.

Some of the many benefits of policy deployment are the following:

- Focuses individual and collective efforts on the vital few activities necessary for organizational success

- Assures enterprise progress through the use of periodic audits

- Helps all employees understand how their efforts contribute to the success of the organization

- Forces decisions to be based on data rather than opinions and anecdotes

- Prevents the strategic plan from being a once-a-year exercise that is never examined until it is time to create next year's plan

- Improves many key company performance measures/ metrics (users have cited 10:1 improvements)

The policy deployment process (see Figure 73) is initiated using an interrelated set of focused questions:

- *Customer-driven master plan.* What is our overall plan for action, both for the long term and the short term? Who are our customers, and what do they need that we can provide? Where do we operate from and why?

- *Mission.* Who are we, and why do we do what we do?

- *Vision.* Who do we want to be and when? How do we want to be viewed by our customers and by society?

- *Strategic (five- to 10-year) plan.* What are we going to do and what resources are we going to allocate to achieve our vision?

- *Tactical (annual) plan.* What are the major components and their target values that comprise our plan?

- *Daily management.* What should we expect in support of our plans from our employees, both individually and collectively, on a daily basis?

- *Improvement initiatives.* What are our most critical problems and how were they identified? What tools should we be using to identify our critical processes and eliminate or reduce customer-related problems?

POPULATIONS VERSUS SAMPLES

A population can be every step in a large organization (an infinite population), every unit of process output (another infinite population or a finite population depending upon the circumstances), or a specific portion of a process output (a finite population of randomly

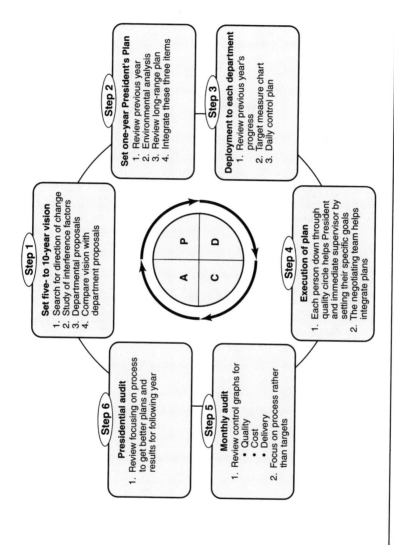

Figure 73 The policy deployment process.

selected units such as a *lot*). In the world of continuous improvement, people try to discover specific facts by collecting sufficient, relevant data and then taking action based on the rigorous analysis of the data. Thus, the data is not collected as an end in itself, but rather as a means of determining the facts that exist behind the data. The facts are most likely to identify the source or sources of specific defects (nonconformances) or defectives (nonconforming product).

One or more items drawn from a population that are intended to provide desired information about the population is called a *sample*. Since a sample is used to estimate the characteristics of an entire population, it should be selected in such a way as to accurately reflect the characteristics of the population from which it is drawn. A commonly used sampling method is to choose any member of the population with equal likelihood. This method is called *random sampling,* and a sample selected by random sampling is referred to as a *random sample.*

Samples are employed in lieu of using all the data available in a population to avoid the high cost of 100 percent inspection and the potential for inspection errors as well as to increase the rate of feedback to process operators.

PRIORITIZATION MATRIX

When a cross-functional team needs to select the best way (be it a method, a tool, a place, an approach) to achieve a specific goal or a task, a prioritization matrix should be employed. This tool is designed to help guide a team through a logical reduction of available options or choices to identify the best one. The reduction process is based on a set of weighted criteria established by the team.

The prioritization matrix uses a simple, L-shaped (two-dimensional) matrix format (see Figure 74). The row headings consist of the various options being considered. The column headings are the criteria to be used for evaluation of the options. After identifying the pertinent criteria, the team agrees on how the criteria should be weighted. This weighting indicates how each of the criteria ranks in importance relative to all the other criteria.

The prioritization matrix is an innovation based on the results of combining two other of the seven management and planning tools: the tree diagram and the L-shaped matrix. Use of the prioritization matrix begins by selecting two sets of data; each set being organized

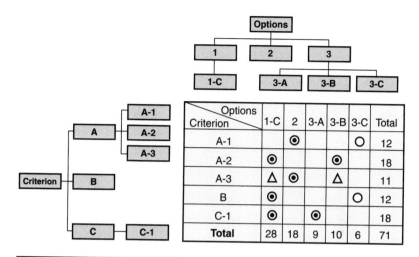

Figure 74 Prioritization matrix.

with a tree diagram. The outputs of the tree diagrams are used to develop both dimensions of the L-shaped matrix that then becomes the prioritization matrix.

PROBLEM-SOLVING PROCESS

Every enterprise that puts into practice a belief in continuous improvement has adopted or adapted some form of Dr. Deming's plan–do–check/study–act cycle.

The very act of using a problem-solving process (PSP), whether it duplicates the one an organization is using or not, assures the organization's management that their focus is on process improvement, not on the creation of one-time fixes for every defect or variation detected by the organization's inspection staff.

Presented in Figure 75 is one such PSP.

PROCESS

A process is a series of sequentially oriented, repeatable tasks or steps having both a beginning and an end and generating a product or service.

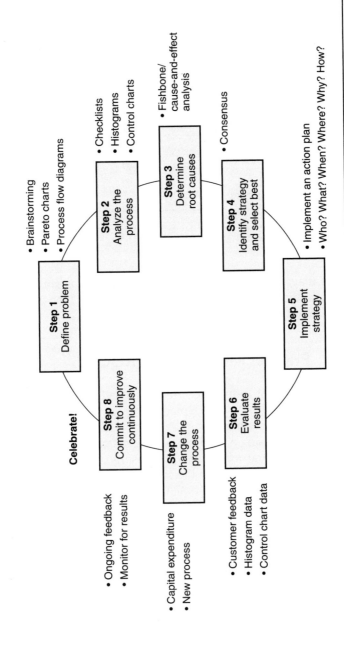

Figure 75 Problem-solving process.

The requirement for standardization or sequential orientation exists in response to the necessity of having a particular series of interrelated tasks or steps occur in the same order each time.

The need for repeatability insures that a sufficient number of occurrences will be recorded, so that performance measures of central tendency and dispersion can be calculated, for example, an average or median and a range or standard deviation.

To be certain that all the members of the cross-functional process improvement team (PIT) charged with process analysis of the process concur on the scope of the process, the team must agree at the outset of their work on what constitutes the beginning and the end of the process.

Finally, for a series of tasks or steps to be considered a process, the resultant of the series must be either a tangible product or an intangible service. A process output results from the coming together of both the known and unknown outputs. Failure to control the process inputs is the cause of failed outputs.

The output, whether tangible or intangible, results from the combining of the input factors: men or women, material, methods, machines, measurements, and environment. These factors are known as the 5 Ms and an E, and are inputs to a cause-and-effect (fishbone) analysis.

Uncontrolled process variation will ultimately result in excessive product and service variation that, in turn, contributes to customer dissatisfaction and loss.

When all of these stipulations have been met then, and only then, is there a process.

PROCESS ANALYSIS

The first phase of process analysis begins by developing a process flowchart. This is followed by creating a list of all the known defects and variances (from design specifications) known to be a result of the process being analyzed. Then each defect and variance is assigned an identification (ID) number or code value.

The second phase calls for the process flowchart to be annotated using the appropriate ID numbers or code values. The unique numbers or values are placed on the process flowchart wherever a specific defect or variance is known to occur, not where it usually gets caught. Figure 76 portrays how the process analysis appears at this point.

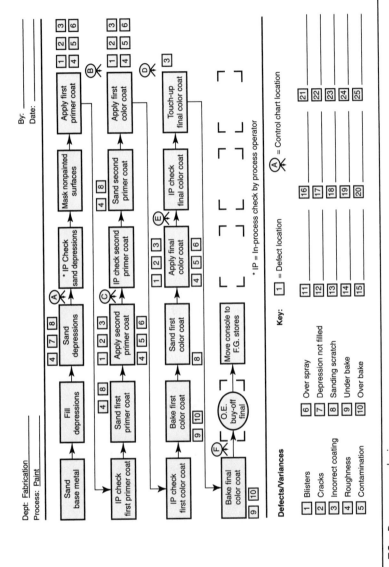

Figure 76 Process analysis.

In the third and final phase of process analysis, the Pareto Principle of *worst first* is employed. Those steps in the process that appear to have the greatest likelihood of generating the most frequent or most costly defects and/or variances should be monitored using statistical control charts and other 7-QC tools.

PROCESS FLOWCHART VERSUS PROCESS MAP

There are a number of different ways to analyze a process. The most common, and one of the most useful, is a graphic tool known as a *process flowchart*. This chart is a series of geometric figures—rectangles, diamonds, circles, or other shapes—arranged typically from left to right, and from top to bottom, connected by lines with arrowheads to show the flow of activity from the beginning (the first task) to the end of the process (the last task).

Process Flowchart

When a new process is being created or an existing process is being analyzed, it is useful to create a process flowchart so that everyone involved, all of the process stakeholders, can see exactly what is supposed to happen from beginning to end without having to imagine it. Everyone may picture what a process flow looks like. However, it may be different from the way others picture it. One way to provide a common perspective or outlook of a process is to graph it as a process flowchart, a linear or one-dimensional, graphical portrayal of a process including points of inspection and test (see Figure 77). It clarifies the interrelationships that exist between tasks or steps and is designed to insure a clear and common vision of a process. (A two-dimensional graphic is a process map.)

In addition, a process flowchart distinguishes between value-added and non-value-added tasks or steps. This attribute facilitates the reduction of process cycle time that subsequently leads to productivity improvement as well as the reduction of defects and variation, and ultimately, the hidden factory.

Traditionally, people have created process flowcharts from the first step to the last step. I don't, and for good reason. The reason is that when people are developing flowcharts, they are looking at their processes in the same way they look at them every single day. This results in a high potential for missing something important.

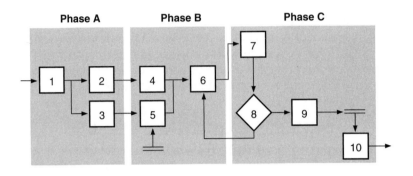

Figure 77   Process flowchart.

What I suggest people do, as they are brought together to create a process flowchart, is start with the end in mind, a term understood by everyone familiar with Stephen Covey's *The 7 Habits of Highly Effective People.*

Begin by defining the last step or the output of the process and then ask the same question sequentially, "What has to happen just before that?" This identifies the predecessor event or events that must take place to satisfy all the needs such that the step you are looking at can take place. Work backwards from the last step to the first step and keep going until someone says, "That's where this whole thing begins." Now you have defined, from the end to the beginning, the process, graphed as a process flowchart.

Some people might question why it should be done this way. Suppose someone were to ask you to recite the alphabet, and you would say *A, B, C, D, E, F, G . . .* without thinking, because you have done it hundreds, perhaps thousands of times. But if you were asked to recite the alphabet backwards, you would probably say *Z* and have to stop and think what happens before that, what letter precedes *Z*. Many people first do it forward to find out what the letter is and then come back and say that the letter before *Z* is *Y*, and the letter before that is *X*, and so on. Working the alphabet backwards makes people look at the alphabet in a way that they have never looked at it before, noticing the interrelationships between predecessor and successor letters (events).

The same psychology of working backwards applies in dealing with processes whether you are dealing with the process of building a home, working with accounts payable, developing a flowchart, understanding a process as it relates to training, or whatever the case may be. Establishing a process flowchart from the last step to the first step is a very strong and powerful way to help people understand what their processes really look like.

Process Map

Once a process flowchart has been created and the PIT is satisfied that it truly reflects the order in which the events take place regarding predecessor and successor events, the next step is to create a process map. This is a two-dimensional, graphic portrayal of a process that incorporates the sequence of process steps with the location, area, or department where the steps occur. Neither the process flowchart nor the process map should be any more detailed than necessary to ensure their practical use.

Beyond the provision of the clear and common vision, the greatest advantage of a process map, when it is annotated with product or service flow rates, is in its use to analyze bottlenecks, locate sources of delay, identify accident sites, and find accumulation of waste.

A process map is created in two dimensions, and the same steps that were identified in developing a process flowchart are used, except instead of just having the flow go from left to right, the people, positions, departments, or functions involved in the process are first listed vertically down the left side of the process map from top to bottom.

For example, the list might be departments *A, B,* and *C;* persons *X, Y,* and *Z;* or departments such as purchasing, operations, and accounting. Then, take the rectangles that were created in the process flowchart and associate them with the various functional areas, departments, or persons listed down the left side of the map. What appears is a series of rectangles being built across the map from left to right and simultaneously moving up and down the vertical axis on the left side of the map, a sawtooth effect with blocks going up, down, and across. Now you see the handoffs from one person to another, one function to another, or one department to another. You can see where queues are being built and the potential for excess work in process (WIP) is being created among the various areas of responsibility listed down the left side.

This provides a clear, visual picture of some of the various process steps you might want to consider reordering or modifying. The objective is to minimize the total number of handoffs that are a part of a process, recognizing that every time there is a handoff, there is the strong potential for an error, an oversight, something left out, a buildup of a queue, the creation of a bottleneck, or the like.

In creating a process map, tremendous insights are gained into what can be done to continuously improve processes (see Figure 78). Remember, the order of the steps may have been absolutely vital at one time, but with changes in technology, people, and responsibilities, what is being done today may no longer be valid, and so you need to periodically assess or review processes. The use of a process map is an excellent way to do that.

In addition to looking at the process flowchart and process map in terms of sequence and handoffs, you can also use these graphics to assess cycle time duration and variation as well as value-added versus non-value-added events or steps in a process. An effective technique is to ask everyone in a room to assess the overall cycle time duration of the process that was just evaluated using a process map or process flowchart. Does it take three hours, five days, 10 weeks, whatever it may be? When an agreement is reached, then each individual step is evaluated. This is accomplished by asking how long each step takes and using the median value as the best choice. When all the individual steps have been estimated, the grand total of all the individual step estimates are summed and then compared to the estimate that the group has already made of the overall process.

What is frequently found is that the sum of the individual steps is only 20 to 30 percent of the overall total. That very quickly presents an image of a great deal of lost and wasted time, costly time that could be used for other important purposes instead of being thrown away. If, for example, a process is estimated to take six weeks, but the sum of the individual components takes a week and

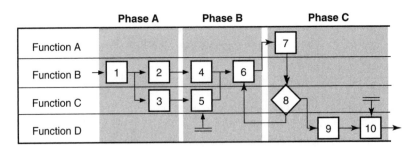

Figure 78   A process map.

a half, it is apparent that some time can be saved. Now, what needs to be done? Where are the barriers, the bottlenecks in the process that can be studied? Where can our departments (for example) share responsibility? Simultaneously sharing responsibilities, instead of passing responsibilities back and forth several times, is an effective way of reducing cycle time. Steps can be eliminated, and days upon days can be banked for use in more important projects.

PROCESS CAPABILITY INDICES
(C_P AND C_{PK})

Overview

Design engineers and process engineers speak two very different languages that, until recently, inhibited their ability to communicate. But now, with the development of two process status indices, the facility to share important design and development as well as manufacturing and assembly information has been considerably enhanced.

Before either of the two indices can be determined, it is mandatory that the subject process be in statistical control. This means that it is necessary to first establish the appropriate control chart and confirm that the process data does not violate any of the rules of control chart interpretation. When it has been confirmed that the process is in control then, and only then, the indices can be applied.

The process capability index, C_P, indicates if a process is capable of consistently providing virtually defect-free product, whereas the mean-sensitive process capability index, C_{PK}, indicates the location of the process natural range relative to product specifications or requirements.

Process Capability Index (C_P)

The process capability index, C_P, is a ratio that relates the tolerance limits of an engineering design specification (the numerator) to the natural range of a process (the denominator). Both entities are expressed in terms of sigma, the process standard deviation.

When C_P is equal to 1.00, then the upper and lower specification limits (the engineering nominal or target value plus or minus the acceptable limits of variation) are identical to the upper and lower natural process limits (the overall process average plus or minus three times sigma). The defect rate associated with this condition is 2700 ppm (parts per million defect opportunities), also known as dpmo (defects per million defect opportunities).

When C_P is greater than 1.00, then the upper and lower spec limits are outside the natural process limits when the process is centered (the engineering nominal value is equal to the overall process average). The greater the value of C_P, the lower the ppm or dpmo.

When C_P is less than 1.00, then the upper and lower spec limits are inside the natural process limits when the process is centered. The smaller the value of C_P, the greater the ppm or dpmo (see Figure 79).

Mean-Sensitive Process Capability Index (C_{PK})

The mean-sensitive process capability index, C_{PK}, is a ratio that quantitatively describes the location of the natural range of a process with respect to the limits of an engineering design specification. The interpretation of C_{PK} values is the same as those for C_P values (see Figure 80).

C_P versus C_{PK}

The use of these indices is straightforward. First, determine if a process is capable at whatever level is desired (1.00, 1.33, 1.50, 1.67, 2.00 or greater). Then, determine at what level the process is performing (the same values). When C_{PK} is equal to C_P, then the process is centered. This means that the lowest possible defect rate for a given C_P has been achieved.

PROCESS CAPABILITY INDICES VERSUS SIX SIGMA (C_P/C_{PK} VERSUS 6σ)

C_P/C_{PK} and 6σ are both performance measures of capability for products, services, and processes. As might be expected, they are mathematically related. Table 3 provides a brief summary of the relationships between C_P/C_{PK} and 6σ as well as percent (proportion) of quality (defect-free) goods and defects per million defect opportunities (dpmo), also known as parts per million (ppm) defect rate.

For example, suppose the upper and lower specification limits of a critical engineering design specification are coincident with the upper and lower natural process limits on a variable control chart. When this is the case, only 93.3 percent of the product is defect-free, the C_{PK} is equal to 0.50, the dpmo is 66,810, and the sigma level is 3.0.

C_P = Ratio of engineering design specification width to natural process range (both expressed in terms of sigma (σ), the process standard deviation

$$C_P = \frac{\text{Design tolerance width}}{\text{Natural process range}}$$

$$C_P = \frac{\text{USL} - \text{LSL}}{\text{UNPL} - \text{LNPL}}$$

Where:

USL, LSL: Upper and lower specification limit

UNPL, LNPL: Upper and lower natural process limit

$$C_P = \frac{\text{"X"}\sigma}{6\sigma}$$

With the objective:

$C_P \geq 2.00$

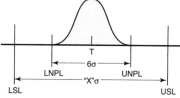

When $C_P \geq 2.00$, a process is capable of producing virtually defect-free product

Figure 79 Process capability index.

C_{PK} = Quantitative location of natural process range with respect to engineering design specification width

C_{PK} = Minimum distance from process average $\overline{\overline{X}}$ to closest specification limit (expressed in terms of sigma [σ], the process standard deviation)

$$C_{PK} = \text{Minimum} \left[\frac{\text{USL} - \overline{\overline{X}}}{3\sigma}, \frac{\overline{\overline{X}} - \text{LSL}}{3\sigma} \right]$$

With the objective: $C_{PK} \geq 2.00$

When $C_{PK} \geq 2.00$, process is performing with virtally defect-free product.

C_{PK} achieves its maximum value, C_P, when the process average ($\overline{\overline{X}}$) is centered on target specification (T), i.e., $C_{PK} \Rightarrow C_P$ as $\overline{\overline{X}} \Rightarrow T$

Remember: C_{PK} cannot exceed C_P

Figure 80 Mean-sensitive process capability index.

Table 3 Relationships between performance measures.

Percent	C_{PK}	dpmo	Sigma
50.0	0.00	500,000	1.5
69.2	0.17	308,500	2.0
84.1	0.33	158,700	2.5
93.3	0.50	66,810	3.0
97.7	0.67	22,750	3.5
99.4	0.83	6,210	4.0
99.87	1.00	1,350	4.5
99.98	1.17	233	5.0
99.997	1.33	32	5.5
99.9997	1.50	3.4	6.0

However, when a variability reduction process has resulted in a much lower standard deviation (a measure of data dispersion) around the process mean (a measure of central tendency), it is quite possible to achieve a 99.9997 percent defect-free product. This is equal to a C_{PK} of 1.50, a 3.4 dpmo, or Six Sigma.

PROCESS CONTROL MATURITY MATRIX (PCMM)

Process-based industries should define, characterize, optimize, validate, and control the quality process before implementing it. What makes an organization stand above others is the depth of rigor to which these five levels of process development are employed. A good way to measure how a company's methodology for process development compares to world-class industries is to place development endeavors on a process control maturity matrix (PCMM).

The PCMM provides a reliable basis for consistent organizational evaluation and serves as a guide to improve and develop processes.

To use the matrix, identify what process development techniques are currently employed and locate them in the matrix. Next, indicate the technique's level of deployment using different colors or shading as noted in Figure 81.

The farther to the right a development activity falls on the matrix, the more rigorous the techniques become and the more valuable the information gleaned. As an activity progresses through the levels, the tools and techniques also increase both in scope and in

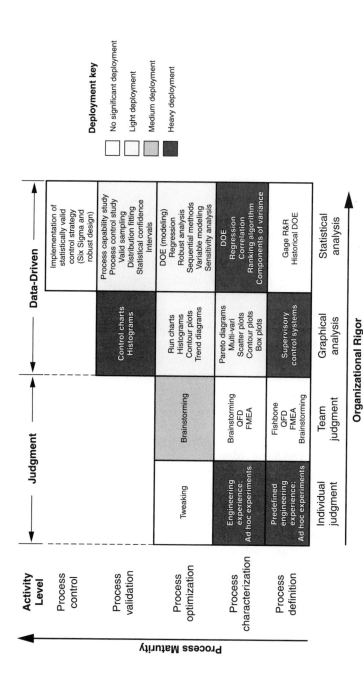

Figure 81 Process control maturity matrix.

Adapted from PCMM, ©1999 by Domain Mfg. Corp. Used with permission.

impact to the bottom line. The most rigorous and comprehensive method, therefore, can be found at the matrix's top right corner, as this method requires a solid foundation to be of value.

World-class organizations operate at medium to heavy deployment toward the right and upper half of the matrix—the stage of statistical analysis. Keeping this in mind, process development leaders can immediately compare their ongoing process development work against the best methods available. Leaders can determine what stage activities are currently in and how much deployment each needs to achieve world-class status.

PROCESS DECISION PROGRAM CHART (PDPC)

The process decision program chart (PDPC) assists cross-functional teams in anticipating events and in developing preventive measures, or countermeasures, for undesired occurrences. It is typically used when a project or task is unique, the situation is complex, and the price of a potential failure is unacceptable.

The PDPC is similar in appearance to an application of the tree diagram. It is designed to lead a cross-functional team through the identification of tasks and paths necessary to achieve a goal as well as the associated subgoals.

The PDPC then leads the team to respond to the questions, "What could go wrong?" and "What unexpected events could occur?" Next, this tool leads the team in the development of countermeasures. The PDPC provides effective contingency planning by mapping out all the conceivable events and then directing attention to where appropriate countermeasures require development.

The PDPC is an effective tool for evaluating a process or activity. It maps out the conceivable activities or actions as well as the associated contingencies in a methodical manner that is easy to explain. It is especially powerful when used in conjunction with other 7-MP tools (see Figure 82).

PROCESS IMPROVEMENT CENTER (PIC)

A process improvement center (PIC) facilitates continuous improvement of a process by bringing together pertinent diagnostics such

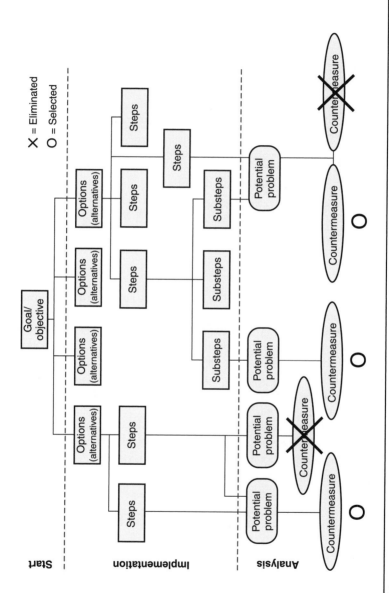

Figure 82 PDPC with countermeasure evaluations.

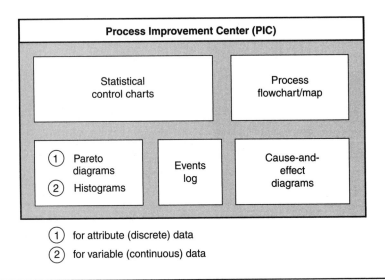

Figure 83   Process improvement center.

as the seven quality control (7-QC) and the seven supplemental (7-SUPP) tools.

Tremendous synergy is achieved by collecting these tools in a single, easy-to-access location in proximity to a process. Process personnel, including process operators, engineers, and supervisors, use a progress center to regularly check the status of a process. This is accomplished through simultaneous review and analysis of all the charts, diagrams, graphs, and logs.

The review and analysis include a check for consistency between each of the various progress center components to ensure that figures noted on one component are in harmony with the others.

Figure 83 offers a process improvement center template.

PROCESS VERSUS SYSTEM

A process is a series of sequentially oriented, repeatable operations having both a beginning and an end that generates either a product or a service:

- *Series.* Two or more steps or operations

- *Sequentially.* Consistent order of steps

- *Repeatable.* Recurring/cycle-oriented

- *Beginning/end.* Agreed—to start and finish steps

- *Product/service.* A tangible or intangible output

After a process has been developed and its operating conditions have been established, six independent factors (each with potential for variation) known in cause-and-effect analysis as the 5 Ms and an E, generate the process output, a dependent variable:

- *Materials.* Variability in raw materials and purchased components

- *Machines.* Process drift, tool wear, mechanical failure, or electrical failure

- *Methods.* Variability in techniques, processes, and procedures

- *Men/women.* Human error of omission, commission, and reversal

- *Measurement.* Bias (lack of accuracy), dispersion (lack of precision), and nonreproducibility (lack of consistency)

- *Environment.* Levels of temperature, humidity, dust, and air flow

- *System.* An interrelated collection of dependent processes, arranged in series and/or parallel, which together constitutes a program, a project, a product, or an entire enterprise

PUSH VERSUS PULL PRODUCTION PROCESSES

The traditional production flow is a push process, that is, a process where an operation produces in accordance with a schedule or plan. This occurs with the product being sent (pushed) to the next operation or to inventory, regardless of need, readiness, and/or demand. This process creates a production environment that is conducive to *muda* (see page 113).

A more logical approach to production flow is the pull process where the product is systematically called upon (pulled) to fill specific customer (internal and external) orders or demands. In this sequence of events, an operation produces only what is taken (pulled) by the next operation downstream.

QUALITY FUNCTION
DEPLOYMENT (QFD)

In the world of business and industry, every organization has customers. Some have only internal customers, some just external customers, and some have both. When a team is working to determine what needs to be accomplished to satisfy or even delight its customer, then the tool of choice is quality function deployment or QFD.

QFD has been referred to by many names; matrix product planning, decision matrices, and customer-driven engineering are just a few examples. Whatever it may be called, QFD is a focused methodology for carefully listening to the voice of the customer and then effectively responding to those needs and expectations.

First developed in Japan in the late 1960s as a form of cause-and-effect analysis (one of the 7-QC tools), QFD was brought to the United States in the early 1980s. It gained its early popularity as a result of numerous successes in the automotive industry.

In QFD, quality is a measure of customer satisfaction with a product or a service. QFD is a structured method that uses the 7-MP tools to quickly and effectively identify and prioritize customers' expectations.

Beginning with the initial matrix, commonly termed the *house of quality* (HOQ) (see Figure 84), the QFD methodology focuses on the most important product or service attributes or qualities. These are composed of customer *wows, wants,* and *musts* (from the Kano model of customer perception versus customer reality). Once they have been prioritized, QFD deploys them to the appropriate organizational function for action (see Figure 85). Thus, QFD is the deployment of customer-driven qualities to the responsible functions of an organization.

There are two major approaches to QFD. The American Supplier Institute advocates a four-phase model while GOAL/QPC uses a 30-matrix model. Depending on what a team's objectives may be, one or the other or a combination of the two models may be the most advantageous approach. Both approaches begin the QFD process using the HOQ.

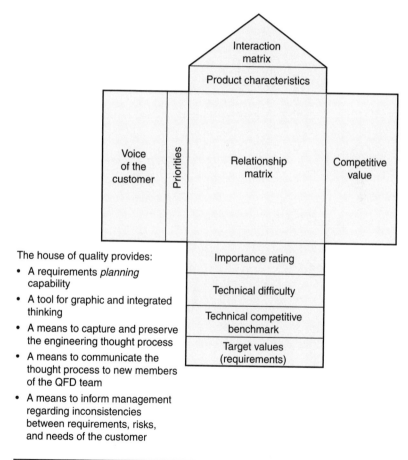

Figure 84   House of quality template and benefits.

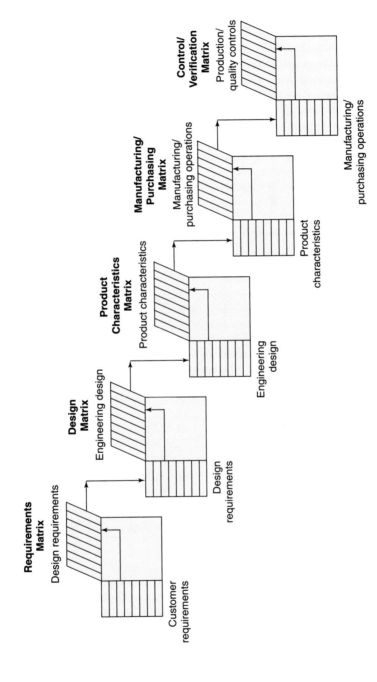

Figure 85 Waterfall relationship of QFD matrices.

Many QFD practitioners claim that using QFD has enabled them to reduce their product and service development cycle times by as much as 75 percent with equally impressive improvements in measured customer satisfaction. Improvements of this magnitude exist throughout America in industry, service organizations, and government agencies.

QUALITY IMPROVEMENT PROCESS (QIP): GETTING STARTED

- Define a process.

- Specify criteria for a critical process.

- Identify all critical processes.

- Prioritize the most critical processes.

- Select the initial set of critical processes that will become the primary focus of the quality improvement process (QIP).

- Identify the process owner and all process stakeholders: supervisors, operators, quality engineers, manufacturing engineers, process engineers, design engineers, suppliers, and customers for each critical process.

- Designate the process owner and all the stakeholders as the process improvement team (PIT) responsible for *QIPing* each critical process.

- Designate the PIT management sponsor, the PIT leader, and the QIP facilitator for each PIT.

- Each PIT creates and requests approval of its charter, and action plan, as well as its process flowchart and process map.

- Each PIT receives its initial training on teaming and QIP.

- Each team initiates its own QIP.

- Each PIT reports on the status of its QIP to their quality council monthly for the first six months and then quarterly.

- PIT reports (approximately 10 minutes) are presented by a different PIT member each time.

- PIT reports include detailed accounts of how the action plan has been implemented, what progress has been achieved, what new actions are contemplated (and why), as well as a listing of training that has been received and to what use it has been put.

- Annually, a symposium consisting of formal presentations by all the PITs with awards for the greatest achievements is held at the corporate office to celebrate the successes of the PITs as an incentive to all employees.

RADAR CHART (SPIDER CHART)

A radar or spider chart, as this tool is sometimes known, is primarily used to analyze and graphically display differences or gaps that exist between various functions or categories (see Figure 86).

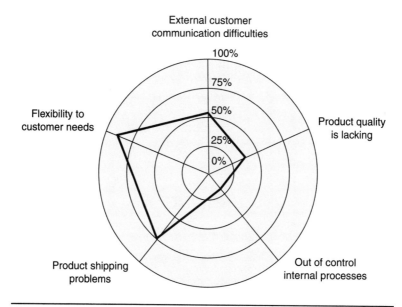

Figure 86 Why are sales down?

A radar chart can show the difference between current status and desired status, where an organization wishes to be evaluated on a number of goals or objectives. It can also show the variation between the views or perceptions of different groups of persons.

Radar charts provide an easy, graphical look at several criteria simultaneously. Knowing where the largest differences are can assist in focusing an organization's efforts to provide the greatest return.

RANDOMIZATION

Randomization is a mathematically oriented technique designed to ensure that every unit in a population has an equal opportunity to be drawn from the population and become a part of a sample. This ensures that, however many samples may be taken from a population, all the samples fairly represent the composition or makeup of the population.

The following are examples of randomization:

1. A sampling of units produced by a process to determine if a process is in statistical control as well as the magnitude of C_P and C_{PK}, the process capability indices.

2. A survey of a company's employee population to ascertain the extent of approval of an entirely new procedure for paid time off.

The application of randomization ensures that the results of a sampling of a population will fairly represent the results that would have been generated had a 100 percent census been conducted. There are major advantages of randomized sampling: it requires less time, costs less, provides fewer opportunities for errors in data collection, and involves fewer personnel as both data collectors and possible respondents.

RANKING

Ranking refers to the assignment of priorities or levels of importance to a set of data. If the data are quantitative, the ranking is based on an analysis of the numbers using a common method of statistical analysis such as Pareto analysis.

If the data happen to be communications or qualitative data, then the ranking is based on a comparison of thoughts or themes using methods such as list reduction, nominal group technique (NGT), or thematic content analysis (TCA).

ROBUST DESIGN

If your organization is in the business of creating unique, one-of-a-kind products or services, like sculptures or paintings, you can skip this section. If both your internal and external customers expect and/or require a high level of predictability, that is, certainty and consistency, with your products and services, then read on.

Picture a room in your home that needs a new wall covering. You select the right quantity of the right paint or wallpaper to take care of the job, but, whoops, you ran out before you finished. Now picture yourself buying an additional can of paint or a roll of wallpaper a week or two following your original purchase. You've even been careful to bring along the manufacturer's code number to ensure that the follow-up purchase would match the original. How are you going to feel when you arrive home and find that the additional material fails to match the original? Not too happy.

There's only one sure way to overcome the tremendous potential for upsets such as this: robust design.

Suppose you've just given a small, balsa wood toy airplane to a young child. Perhaps you've suggested that he or she try to make the airplane fly as far as possible (a dependent variable) but with some added stipulations. Rather than just adjusting the features of the airplane to maximize the distance flown, you also want to minimize the deviation from flight to flight. For example, you won't be satisfied when the average distance flown after 10 or so throws is 30 feet if the shortest flight is 15 feet and the longest is 45 feet (±50 percent). What you'd really like to have is an average flight of 30 feet with the shortest flight being 27 feet and the longest at 33 feet (±10 percent). This certainly leads to the conclusion that what is needed is a design of experiments (DOE).

So you explain to the child that there are some airplane features (independent variables) that influence the performance of the airplane. Some of the features he or she can control such as, the location of the wing in its slot in the body of the airplane (level one = wing in the forward position, level two = wing in the rearward position), the height of the vertical stabilizer (level one = normal position, level two = turned so the top of the tail faces the nose of the airplane), and the use of additional ballast (paper clip) on the nose of the airplane (level one = no clip, level two = clip added). These are referred to as the controllable factors.

In addition to the controllable factors, there are other factors influencing the performance of the airplane that should be considered, but which cannot be controlled for one reason or another. Those reasons could include cost, difficulty in making level changes, a lack of awareness of relevance, or even the presence of a factor. These are called the uncontrollable, or noise, factors.

In this illustration, two examples of uncontrollable/noise factors are: launch energy (level one = airplane thrown with very little force, level two = airplane thrown with great force), and launch angle (level one = airplane thrown slightly upward, level two = airplane thrown horizontally, and level three = airplane thrown slightly downward).

Level selection for uncontrollable/noise factors is based on maximum and minimum values anticipated in actual settings. There is no need to study the effect of a factor level that goes beyond (either higher or lower) what could normally be expected to occur. For example, in the case of the balsa wood airplane, it would not be necessary to be concerned about a launch energy beyond the ability of an average child.

At this point, it should be noted that factor levels are not limited to only two; however, the more levels you desire to study, the greater the number of experimental runs required. Naturally, this drives up the cycle time and the cost of conducting a DOE.

Whether you are talking about a product or a process, a robust design has been achieved when the undesirable influences of the uncontrollable/noise factors have been overcome by setting the controllable factors at their optimal levels and, in so doing, ensuring that the performance of the product or process is consistent, uniform, and predictable.

In the example of the balsa wood airplane, this means that the goal of creating a robust design has been achieved. Thus, the airplane is now capable of a maximum average distance flown with a minimum deviation from flight to flight. This was attained by overcoming the undesirable influences of the uncontrollable/noise factors through selection of the optimal levels of the controllable factors.

Credit is due to Dr. Genichi Taguchi, executive director of the American Supplier Institute in Allen Park, Michigan, and a world-renowned consultant, who not only popularized the concepts of robust design and the quality loss function but who also created the concepts of the inner–outer array tableau and the signal-to-noise ratio (both used in the development of a robust design of experiments).

ROOT CAUSE ANALYSIS

Root cause analysis is an advanced form of a problem-solving process. The process flowchart shown in Figure 87 introduces the sequentially oriented steps of root cause analysis.

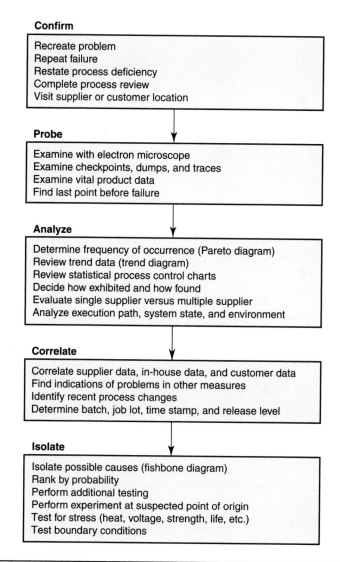

Confirm
Recreate problem
Repeat failure
Restate process deficiency
Complete process review
Visit supplier or customer location

Probe
Examine with electron microscope
Examine checkpoints, dumps, and traces
Examine vital product data
Find last point before failure

Analyze
Determine frequency of occurrence (Pareto diagram)
Review trend data (trend diagram)
Review statistical process control charts
Decide how exhibited and how found
Evaluate single supplier versus multiple supplier
Analyze execution path, system state, and environment

Correlate
Correlate supplier data, in-house data, and customer data
Find indications of problems in other measures
Identify recent process changes
Determine batch, job lot, time stamp, and release level

Isolate
Isolate possible causes (fishbone diagram)
Rank by probability
Perform additional testing
Perform experiment at suspected point of origin
Test for stress (heat, voltage, strength, life, etc.)
Test boundary conditions

Figure 87 Steps for a root cause analysis.

RUN CHART

A run chart (or trend chart) is a line chart that permits the study of data over a specified period of time. The data can be either attribute/discrete data or continuous/variable data. After observations have been made and the associated data recorded, the data points are plotted and connected as a run chart (see Figures 88 and 89). The resulting line allows examination for trends or patterns such as cycles or shifts in magnitude. The chart is typically oriented with time plotted on the X (horizontal) axis, and the data plotted on the Y (vertical) axis.

The average value of the original input data is calculated and plotted as a horizontal line across the specified time period. The average line is then used to estimate the orientation of the data; that is, is it reasonably constant with minor data dispersion evenly balanced above and below the average line, or is there an upward or downward trend? A median line is sometimes used as the centerline because it provides a nonparametric (not dependent on the distribution) estimate of the process centerline.

A run chart is the beginning of a (statistical) control chart. All that needs to be added are the upper and lower natural process limits which are calculated as plus/minus three standard deviations based on the original input data.

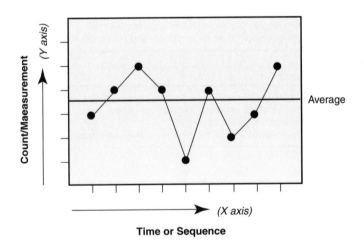

Figure 88   Run chart—example 1.

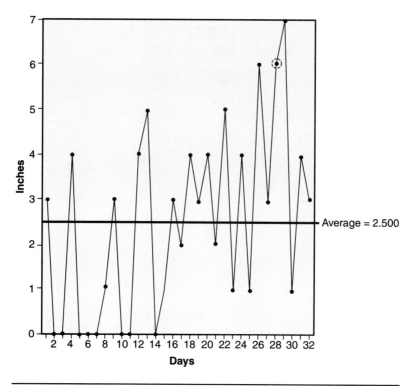

Figure 89 Run chart—example 2.

S

SAMPLING

Sampling is the selection of a set of elements from a population or product lot. Sampling is frequently used because population data are often impossible, impractical, or too costly to collect. When this is the case, a sample is used to draw conclusions or make inferences about the parent population from which the sample is drawn.

When used in conjunction with randomization, samples provide virtually identical characteristics relative to those of the population from which the sample was drawn. Users of sampling are cautioned, however, that there are three categories of sampling error: bias (lack of accuracy), dispersion (lack of precision), and nonreproducibility (lack of consistency). These are easily accounted for by knowledgeable practitioners. A pictorial representation of the types of sampling error is presented in Figure 90.

Determinations of sample sizes for specific situations are readily obtained through the selection and application of the appropriate mathematical equation. All that is needed to determine the minimum sample size is to specify: if the data are continuous (variable) or discrete (attribute), if the population is finite or infinite, what confidence level is desired/specified, the magnitude of the maximum allowable error (due to bias, dispersion and/or nonreproducibility), and the likelihood of occurrence of a specific event. Figure 91 summarizes this information.

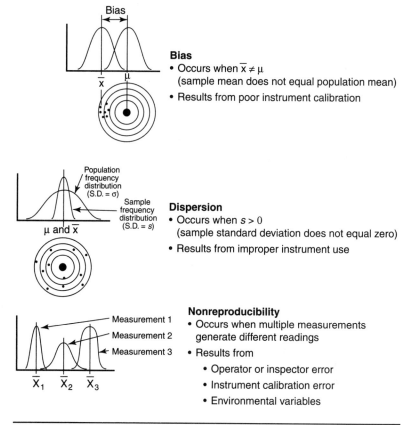

Figure 90 Types of sampling error.

SCATTER ANALYSIS

The most basic form of a design of experiments (DOE) is a graphical analysis of two types of data. One type of data is treated as being independent, and the other is considered as being dependent, a type of data whose magnitude is somehow mathematically related to the value of the first type. When these two types of data are plotted on an X–Y coordinate graph, the resulting pattern of bivariate (x, y) data points is referred to as a scatter diagram or scatter plot.

Continuous Data		
n:N Relationship	**Population (N)**	**Equation**
$n \leq 0.05N$	Infinite	$n = \dfrac{Z^2 s^2}{E^2}$
$n > 0.05N$	Finite	$n = \dfrac{Z^2 s^2}{E^2 + \dfrac{Z^2 s^2}{N}}$
Discrete Data		
n:N Relationship	**Population (N)**	**Equation**
$n \leq 0.05N$	Infinite	$n = \dfrac{Z^2 p\,(1 - p)}{E^2}$
$n > 0.05N$	Finite	$n = \dfrac{Z^2 p\,(1 - p)}{E^2 + \dfrac{Z^2 p\,(1 - p)}{N}}$

Where:
n = Sample size
N = Population size
Z = Number of standard deviations corresponding to a desired confidence level (Z = 1.96 for CL = 95%)
s = Magnitude of standard deviation
E = Maximum allowable error
p = Likelihood of occurrence of a specific event

Figure 91   Sample size formulas.

Scatter analysis, the interpretation of a diagram or plot, is used to determine the extent to which the two types of data may be related as well as the orientation of the relationship. The extent of the relationship is defined as falling between zero and one while the orientation can be either positive or negative, from +1 to −1.

If, as a result of a scatter analysis, it is apparent that the magnitude of the dependent variable is increasing or decreasing in the same direction as the independent variable, then this is a case of a positive relationship. If the scatter analysis indicates that the dependent variable is decreasing when the independent variable is increasing, or vice versa, then this is a case of a negative relationship. The positive or negative orientation describes the plus or minus value of the slope of a line that best describes any existing relationship between the two variables.

Figure 92 portrays several scatter patterns.

Figure 93 is an example of scatter analysis. The bivariate data in the aircraft are accurate but provide no clues to which airlines are doing well and which ones aren't. Figure 94 paints a graphic picture of which airlines are in trouble with respect to their costs.

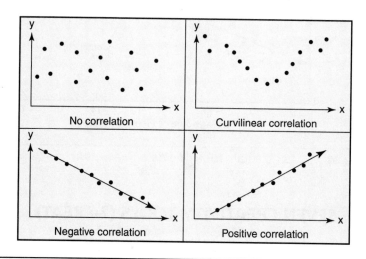

Figure 92 Data correlation patterns for scatter analysis.

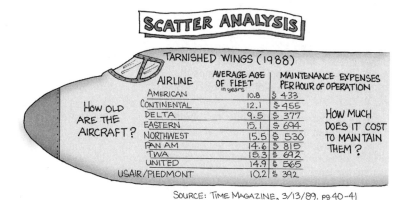

AIRLINE	AVERAGE AGE OF FLEET in years	MAINTENANCE EXPENSES PER HOUR OF OPERATION
AMERICAN	10.8	$ 433
CONTINENTAL	12.1	$455
DELTA	9.5	$ 377
EASTERN	15.1	$ 694
NORTHWEST	15.5	$ 530
PAN AM	14.6	$ 815
TWA	15.3	$ 692
UNITED	14.9	$ 565
USAIR/PIEDMONT	10.2	$ 392

TARNISHED WINGS (1988)

HOW OLD ARE THE AIRCRAFT?

HOW MUCH DOES IT COST TO MAINTAIN THEM?

SOURCE: TIME MAGAZINE, 3/13/89, pg. 40-41

Figure 93 Average maintenance costs and aircraft ages for various airlines.

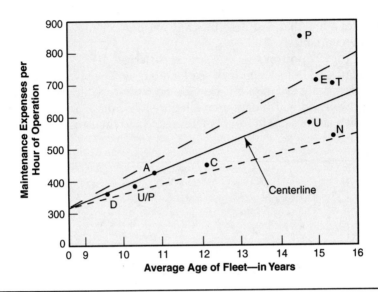

Figure 94 Scatter diagram for airline data.

SEVEN CREATIVITY TOOLS (7-CREAT)

Which of the creative tools should be applied when your team wants to achieve each of the following:	The tool of choice should be the following:
Find a solution to a problem by visualizing and evaluating its various elements and underlying structure.	Heuristic redefinition
Produce and evaluate a maximum quantity of potential ideas in a minimum amount of time by fully using the collective creativity plus the knowledge and experience of a multidisciplinary team.	Classical brainstorming
Take ideas produced by other team members and develop them further, especially when a team is large, team dynamics require an unusual approach, or when a problem requires additional analytical thinking.	Brainstorming 635
Generate unusual ideas and break established patterns of thinking, thus allowing a team to identify more creative ideas and solutions to problems.	Imaginary brainstorming

continued

continued

Which of the creative tools should be applied when your team wants to achieve each of the following:	The tool of choice should be the following:
Generate new ideas by thinking outside the box, stimulate ideas by simple analogy from inventions that share similar principles to the problem or concern being studied, and search for new ideas by examining as many other fields as possible.	Word and picture association
Use a multiphase, systematic, and structured approach for idea generation to find ingenious, creative materials from other fields for application to an immediate problem or concern, especially when each phase can be completed by the same or separate teams.	TILMAG
Identify all practical solutions to highly complex or extremely significant problems. Team members must possess extensive knowledge about the specific technology in question, possess sharp analytical thinking, and have the ability to precisely define a problem and its components.	Morphological box

SEVEN HABITS (7-HABITS)

Dr. Stephen R. Covey in *The Seven Habits of Highly Effective People* lists the following traits to improve the quality of life:

1. Be proactive and accept responsibility to choose your best response to stimuli.

2. Begin with the end in mind by starting each day or task with a clear understanding of where you want to go and how you're going to get there.

3. Put first things first by organizing and managing time and events according to your personal priorities established in Habit 2.

4. "Think win–win" is founded on your personal character and views of life as a series of cooperative opportunities to achieve mutually beneficial solutions.

5. Seek first to understand, then to be understood when you want to communicate effectively with people who are important to you.

6. Synergize to maximize the value of the differences between people, that is, the mental, the emotional, and the physiological differences.

7. Sharpen the saw to preserve and enhance your greatest asset—you—by implementing a balanced, systematic program for self-renewal in each important area of your life.

SEVEN MANAGEMENT AND PLANNING TOOLS (7-MP)

Just as with the seven quality control (7-QC) tools, each of the seven management and planning (7-MP) tools was created independently, that is, by different persons in different places at different times for different purposes. One of the beauties of both the 7-QC and the 7-MP tools is that while each has a specific purpose and can be used independently, that is, without regard to any of the other tools, the output data from one tool can and should become the input data to another. Within the family of the 7-QC tools, for example, the output of Pareto analysis frequently becomes the input to a cause-and-effect analysis. And when there is some question as to the existence of a relationship between two variables in a cause-and-effect analysis, then a scatter analysis is employed to provide necessary clarification, that is, verify if one of the variables is dependent and the other independent.

Which of the 7-MP tools should be applied when your team wants to achieve each of the following:	The tool of choice should be the following:
Reduce a collection of ideas to a much smaller quantity of themes.	Affinity analysis
From a collection of themes, determine the input and output relationships and then identify which themes are drivers and which are outcomes.	Interrelationship digraph (ID)
Compare one collection of ideas with another to determine the extent of their interrelationships.	Matrix analysis
Compare the attributes of a collection of alternative solutions using a selected set of criteria to determine which of the solutions is preferred to achieve a particular objective.	Prioritization matrix

continued

continued

Which of the 7-MP tools should be applied when your team wants to achieve each of the following:	The tool of choice should be the following:
Separate a top-level idea into its next-level component parts and then divide these into their next-level component parts, and so on.	Tree diagram
Given an idea, identify the various possible approaches that might achieve the idea, with each approach to include requirements, potential failures, possible countermeasures, and the likelihood of success or failure for each countermeasure, thus resulting in determination of the optimal approach to achieve the idea.	Process decision program chart (PDPC)
Sequentially plot a group of events using series and parallel relationships to portray the network of events with its critical path as well as the start and finish times for each event.	Activity network diagram (AND)

SEVEN QUALITY CONTROL TOOLS (7-QC)

Which of the 7-QC tools should be applied when your team wants to achieve each of the following:	The tool of choice should be the following:
Graphically collect data, either attribute or variable, relative to its frequency of occurrence.	Data tables (check sheets or tally sheets)
Graphically record brainstorming the potential cause(s) of a selected effect, either positive or negative.	Cause-and-effect analysis
Graphically plot frequency of occurrence of continuous (variable) data within specific class intervals.	Histograms
Graphically plot frequency of occurrence of discrete (attribute) data from the greatest value on the left to the least value on the right.	Pareto analysis
Graphically plot bivariate data points *(x, y)* to determine if one variable is mathematically related to the other.	Scatter analysis
Graphically plot data, either attribute or variable, as averages or individuals, to ascertain the presence of positive or negative trends.	Trend analysis (graphs or run charts)
Graphically plot data, either attribute or variable, as averages or individuals, to ascertain if a process is in statistical control.	Control charts

SEVEN SUPPLEMENTAL TOOLS (7-SUPP)

Which of the supplemental tools should be applied when your team wants to achieve each of the following:	The tool of choice should be the following:
Use an inspection or test form to tally quantities of various types of defects as well as to specify their locations relative to unit geometry.	Defect map
Create a detailed chronological listing of those process-related events that differ from the norm and that should be used as a problem-solving tool when a control chart, histogram, or Pareto analysis indicate the presence of an abnormality.	Events log
Convert a population or a sample from a single collection of heterogeneous data into two or more subgroups of homogeneous data, for example, convert all defects into two classes—major and minor defects, or convert all students into those with As, Bs, or Cs, and so on.	Data stratification
Apply a formalized administrative process to ensure that each and every unit in a population has an equal opportunity for selection or inclusion in a sample. The team can use random number tables, computer-generated random numbers, and/or 10/20-sided dies.	Randomization
Graphically depict a process, linear or nonlinear, indicating the sequence of steps as well as the input and output for each step. The flowchart portrays only the process steps while the map indicates location, area, or department as well.	Process flowchart or map
Incorporate the use of a display board located in proximity to a specific process. This display board contains a current control chart, process flowchart or map, Pareto analysis (for attribute data) or histogram (for variable data), events log, and any other process-related data.	Progress center
Use a statistically based procedure to determine sample size and to select units from a population of units for purposes such as inspection and test.	Statistical sampling

SEVEN TEAM SUPPORT TOOLS (7-TEAM)

Which of the team support tools should be applied when the team wants to achieve each of the following:	The tool of choice should be the following:
Compare items on a list using a standard or benchmark previously agreed to by the team.	Forced choice
Prioritize a brief list of ideas by evaluating each idea on the list with every other idea.	Pairwise ranking
Determine the highest priority ideas within a long list of items, but the team is large and needs to avoid any win–lose situations.	Multivoting
Reduce a long list of ideas to a shorter, more manageable size or, alternatively, assign operational priorities to each item on a long list.	List reduction
Avoid any of the following: • Pressure toward team conformity • Effect of senior status • Going off on tangents • Getting too narrowly focused • Being unwilling to say something that sounds completely foolish	Nominal group technique (NGT)
Organize a large number of ideas using the creative rather than the logical part of the brain by working with colors and images to promote visualization of ideas.	Mind mapping
Reach consensus on subjects of consequence by merging ideas, conclusions, or beliefs whether participants are in the same room or geographically dispersed and which enables team members to participate anonymously.	Delphi method

SIX SIGMA (6σ)

Consider a product: its performance is determined by the margin between the actual characteristic values of design requirements and its manufactured parts. These characteristics are produced by factory processes and their suppliers.

Every process attempts to reproduce its characteristic values identically from unit to unit, but variations do occur. Processes that use real-time feedback have small variation, but other processes may have large variation.

Variation of a process is measured in standard deviations (sigma) from the process average. Normal process variation is considered to be plus or minus three sigma.

Under normal conditions, about 2700 parts per million (ppm) defect opportunities will occur outside the normal variation. This, by itself, does not appear disconcerting, but a product containing only 1500 parts will have 4.05 defects per unit. This would result in fewer than two units out of every hundred going through the entire manufacturing process without a defect.

It can be seen that for a product to be built virtually defect-free, it must be designed to accept characteristics that are significantly more than plus or minus three sigma from the process mean.

It can be demonstrated that a design that can accept twice the normal variation of the process, that is, plus or minus six sigma, can be expected to have not more than 3.4 ppm defects for each characteristic, when the process mean shifts by plus or minus 1.5 sigma, and the spread extends to 4.5 sigma (see Figure 95).

In the same case of a product containing 1500 parts, only 0.0051 defects per unit would be expected. This would mean that 995 units out of 1,000 would go through the entire manufacturing process without a defect.

The goal is to design a product that will accept maximum variation and processes that produce minimum variation, ultimately reaching zero defects. Many other world-class organizations have followed Motorola's lead in setting the objective to achieve a plus or

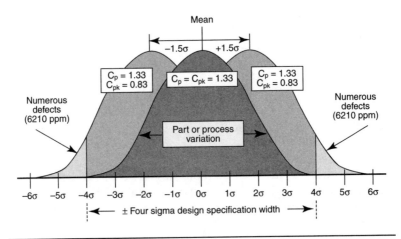

Figure 95   Illustration of 1.5 sigma shift.

minus six sigma capability. By the way, a process capability index (C_P or C_{PK}) of 2.00 is equal to six sigma.

SIX SIGMA PROBLEM-SOLVING MODEL AND TOOLS

Overview

This model is presented in two formats. Figure 96 is a process flow-chart that describes the sequence of activities and decisions necessary to solve process-related problems effectively and efficiently. Figure 97 duplicates the first, but with the addition of the names of the most useful tools and/or methods to apply.

The model was originally based on the Deming/Shewhart plan–do–check–act cycle, but has been modified to fit the Six Sigma define–measure–analyze–improve–control model. The earliest version of the model was created in 1985 as part of a seminar I presented to a client.

When the model is introduced as part of a seminar, the first figure is examined and discussed to gain consensus from the course participants regarding the rationale of step selection and arrangement. When consensus is achieved on the first figure, the second figure is presented to demonstrate how each tool and/or method in the bottom half of each box is employed to ensure the quickest and easiest completion of each step. In addition, the class members see how the output of a tool in one step becomes the input to a tool in the subsequent step.

Phase One

Figure 96 is best understood by beginning its examination at the top left and moving to the right or left by following the arrowheads. Phase One of the model starts with the identification of both internal (operational) and external (customer) problems. This can be as simple as developing a comprehensive listing of problems drawn from a specific department, multiple departments (cross-functional), a single division, multiple divisions, or from the entire company.

Once the list has been developed, it should be prioritized by ranking the problems. The problem at the top of the list is identified as the primary problem. The next step is to identify the process or processes associated with the primary problem. Then it is necessary

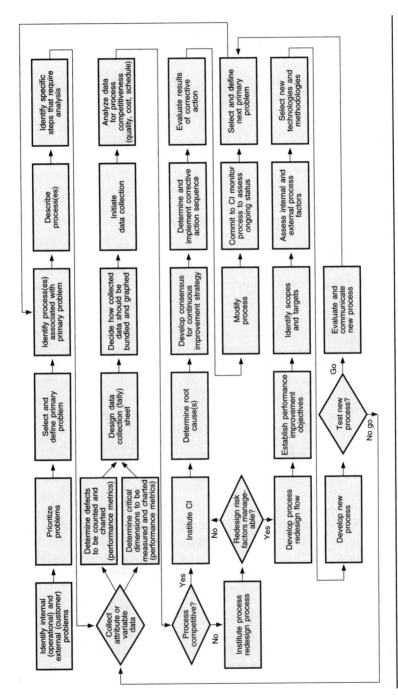

Figure 96 Six Sigma problem-solving model using continous improvement and process redesign.

©2003 by ReVelle Solutions.

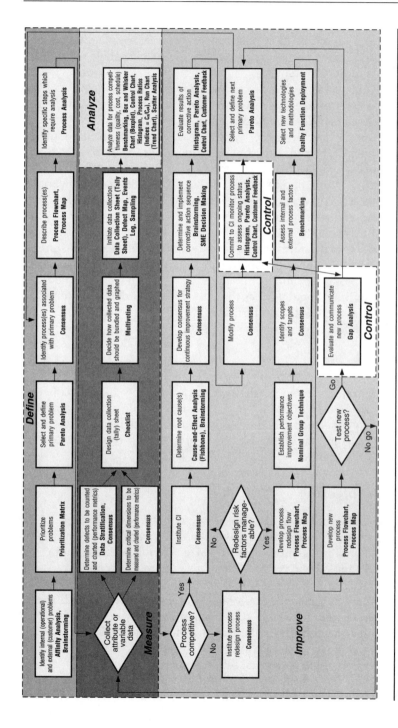

Figure 97 Six Sigma DMAIC problem-solving model using continuous improvement and process redesign.

©2003 by ReVelle Solutions.

to clearly describe each selected process. Now magnification is increased, so model users can identify the specific steps within each process requiring analysis.

At this point in the Six Sigma problem-solving sequence, it is necessary to make a decision whether to collect attribute data or variable data. Whatever decision is reached, the next step is to decide what performance metrics will be used throughout the remainder of the problem-solving sequence. If the decision is to collect attribute data, then it is necessary to determine which defects should be counted and charted. If the decision is to collect variable data, then it is necessary to determine which critical dimensions to measure and chart.

At this point, the data collection sheet (or tally sheet) is designed as a user-friendly form that is easy to complete and easy to summarize. Then, following appropriate discussions, it is necessary to decide how the collected and summarized data should be bundled and graphed. Bundling describes the numerator and denominator of the ratio to be used as the performance metric, for example, defects per million defect opportunities.

Phase Two

As might be expected, Phase Two starts with the collection of sufficient data to be representative of the entire problem. When this data has been collected, it is time to initiate data analysis to determine just how competitive the process really is with respect to quality, cost, and schedule.

Phase Three

Phase Three begins with a question: is the process competitive? If the decision is in the affirmative, then you track Phase Three-A in which continuous improvement (kaizen) of the process is appropriate and should be instituted. CI begins with the determination of the root causes of the original problem.

Developing a consensus strategy for CI follows the identification of the root causes. Next, a corrective action sequence is determined and implemented. Evaluation of the data generated and collected subsequent to the introduction of the correction actions should reveal the wisdom of the corrective action sequence.

When the results justify doing so, the next step is to modify the process in whatever way the newly collected data indicate is appropriate. At this point a commitment must be made to CI and to monitor the process to assess its ongoing status. Without this commitment, the likelihood of the process reverting to its original status is virtually 100 percent. The final step in Phase Three-A is to select and define the next problem to be addressed, thus returning our attention to Phase One.

Returning to the beginning of Phase Three, if a decision is made that the process is not competitive with respect to quality, cost, and schedule, then follow Phase Three-B, which begins with instituting the process redesign sequence. This brings us to still another decision point where it must be decided whether or not the redesign risk factors are manageable.

If it is determined that they are not, then return to Phase Three-A. If, on the other hand, the redesign risk factors are assessed to be manageable, then the next step is to establish specific performance improvement objectives. This is followed by quantifying the target values.

Phase Three-B continues with the assessment of germane or pertinent internal and external process factors. These are the factors that have a high potential of contributing to the success or failure of the process redesign effort.

At this point, focus on the selection of new technologies and/or methods that may replace those used in the existing process. Now organize the old technologies or methods that will be retained as well their new counterparts to develop the new process. The new process is tested using all the steps of Phase Two to decide whether or not it is as good or better than the original process. If the decision is favorable, communicate it to all the process stakeholders and return to the final step of Phase Three-A. If the decision is a no-go, then return to the first step in Phase Two.

Figure 97 duplicates Figure 96 with two significant additions. Figure 97 also provides the names of the tools and/or methods most appropriate to conduct the prescribed activity within each step efficiently and effectively. The Six Sigma DMAIC model has been superimposed on Figure 96, the author's model.

Conclusion

Whenever a process improvement team (PIT) or a team member desires further explanation or discussion on either the Six Sigma problem-solving model or any of the tools and/or methods, the PIT team leader is empowered and encouraged to contact a knowledgeable internal or external statistical consultant to obtain whatever technical assistance may be needed. Depending on your organization and its extent of involvement with Six Sigma, this person might be a master Black Belt, a Black Belt, or even a Green Belt.

SIX SIGMA VERSUS TQM

While Six Sigma and TQM share the use of many tools such as Pareto analysis, cause-and-effect analysis, histograms, process maps, scatter analysis, tally sheets, and run/trend charts, the commonality ends there.

For example, while process improvement teams (PITs) using TQM identify their own projects based on their limited perspective of what seems to be critical, PITs that are part of a Six Sigma initiative receive their project assignments from higher up in their organizations where broader knowledge of project criticality is available and the projects have been prioritized.

In addition, Six Sigma places much greater emphasis on the voice of the customer than does TQM. The sigma level of quality provides necessary guidance in this regard. Six Sigma makes much greater use of statistical software and rigorous statistical methods than does TQM.

Unlike TQM, Six Sigma fully defines a variety of organizational roles and responsibilities as well as minimum training and experience requirements for personnel involved in their organization's Six Sigma initiative.

SIX SIGMA: DMAIC MODEL

While most quality practitioners are familiar with the plan–do–check–act process improvement cycle first developed by Walter Shewhart in the1930s and popularized by W. Edwards Deming in the 1970s and 1980s, many of these same quality professionals are not as conversant with the more recent DMAIC process improvement cycle developed in association with Six Sigma.

DMAIC, spoken as dee-may-ick, stands for *define, measure, analyze, improve,* and *control.* The Six Sigma methodology requires that process improvement teams (PITs) with trained process stakeholders, process owners, Green Belts, and/or Black Belts use this five-phase approach to problem solving and/or process improvement.

Once a prioritized list of potential projects has been selected, a PIT is formed to work the most critical or important problems first. Criticality or importance is usually expressed in terms of financial savings (cost avoidance), customer satisfaction, and product or service quality.

The purpose of the *define* phase is to scope out the project and obtain relevant process and customer data. The PIT's project charter is developed and the process flowchart or process map are created during this phase.

The purpose of the *measure* phase is to acquire *as is* process information to create baseline data.

The purpose of the *analyze* phase is to examine the data generated or collected in the measure phase so as to identify root causes of the problem being studied.

The purpose of the *improvement* phase is to create, test, and implement corrective actions that positively respond to known problem causes.

The purpose of the *control* phase is to sustain whatever improvements were made by requiring conformance to prescribed directives resulting from the improvement phase.

SIX SIGMA: ROLES AND RESPONSIBILITIES

Within the context of Six Sigma, there are a variety of specific but closely related roles. Each role has a well-defined set of position expectations and requires satisfactory completion of necessary training requirements.

The following presents a brief summary of these position expectations (PE) and training requirements (TR) for each role.

Black Belts

- *PE:* Selects, leads, executes, completes, and reports progress on critical projects. Teaches PIT members. Mentors Green Belts. Transfers knowledge to other Black Belts.

- *TR:* Minimum of four weeks covering continuous improvement tools, DMAIC, and advanced statistical software.

Champions

- *PE:* Selects and mentors Black Belts. Eliminates barriers for Black Belts and ensures the availability of necessary resources. Communicates PIT progress to director of quality.

- *TR:* Minimum of one week covering continuous improvement tools, DMAIC, and basic statistical software.

Council of Champions

- *PE:* Determines organizational goals and objectives as well as key business drivers. Selects champions and directors of quality.

- *TR:* Minimum of one day covering strategy, continuous improvement tools, DMAIC, and Six Sigma success stories.

Directors of Quality

- *PR:* Deploys Six Sigma throughout the organization. Assists PIT sponsors to identify their organizational goals and objectives to insure they are aligned with those of the Council of Champions.

- *TR:* Black Belt or equivalent.

Green Belts

- *PR:* Assigned to work on less-than-critical projects, usually within their immediate function. Can be PIT members on critical projects led by a Black Belt.

- *TR:* Minimum of one week covering continuous improvement tools, DMAIC, and basic statistical software.

Master Black Belts

- *PR:* Selects, trains, and mentors Black Belts. Provides liaison between Black Belts, director of quality, and council of champions. Subject matter expert on all Six Sigma tools, software, concepts, and strategy.

- *TR:* At least two weeks beyond Black Belts to include leadership and management skills as well as accounting and finance.

Process Owners

- *PR:* Responsible for all aspects of their processes including quality and quantity of both process inputs and outputs. Usually, a PIT member responsible for maintaining project improvements at the conclusion of DMAIC.

- *TR:* One to three days on continuous improvement tools, DMAIC, and basic statistical software.

Process Stakeholders

- *PR:* Monitor status of all aspects of their processes. May provide physical and/or other input to insure planned process flow.

- *TR:* Same as process owners.

Process Improvement Team Members

- *PR:* Work on assignments made by PIT leaders (Black Belts and Green Belts).

- *TR:* Same as process owners.

Sponsors

- *PR:* May also be champions. Provide necessary resources in support of PITs.

- *TR:* Same as champions.

SOCIO-TECHNICAL RELATIONSHIPS

The TQM puzzle has many pieces, but it is not always obvious how or where they fit together. Some people take years to learn through reading and organizational experimentation. Others never learn and, unfortunately, still others believe they've learned when in fact they haven't really put it all together.

For the most part, TQM failures occur when its champion and his or her staff don't truly understand the details of the socio-technical relationships that underlie any attempt to install TQM within the existing culture of an organization. Because of these and other

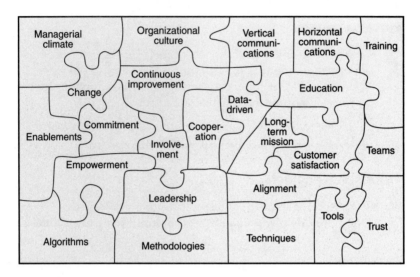

Figure 98   The TQM puzzle.

inadequacies associated with TQM, the need for something better resulted in the creation and growth of Six Sigma.

The three primary aspects of TQM (social, managerial, and technical) are closely intertwined. Thus, they must be recognized as the underpinnings of any TQM successes.

The identities of the multitude of pieces of the TQM puzzle are similar from organization to organization; however, the precise fit will vary according to the organization's culture and industry. Figure 98 illustrates how pieces of the TQM puzzle can be joined in an organization.

STATISTICAL ENGINEERING

Statistical engineering refers to a body of knowledge, all of which is related to an approach to design of experiments (DOE) created and popularized by Dorian Shainin. It is a collection of DOE-related tools and techniques that are especially well suited to solving production problems.

Prior to his death in 2000, Mr. Shainin, working with his two sons, consistently solved problems that had previously been thought to be without a solution. Armed only with his knowledge of statistical engineering and his vast experience, he had successfully come to the rescue of innumerable enterprises that believed that there was no solution to at least one of their problems.

STATISTICAL QUALITY CONTROL VERSUS STATISTICAL PROCESS CONTROL (SQC VERSUS SPC)

In 1974 Dr. Kaoru Ishikawa brought together a collection of process improvement tools in his text *Guide to Quality Control*. Known around the world as the seven quality control (7-QC) tools, they are:

- Cause-and-effect analysis
- Check sheets/tally sheets
- Control charts
- Graphs
- Histograms
- Pareto analysis
- Scatter analysis

In addition to the basic 7-QC tools, there are also some additional tools known as the seven supplemental (7-SUPP) tools:

- Data stratification
- Defect maps
- Events logs
- Process flowcharts/maps
- Progress centers
- Randomization
- Sample size determination

Statistical quality control (SQC) is the application of the 14 statistical and analytical tools (7-QC and 7-SUPP) to monitor process *outputs* (dependent variables). Statistical process control (SPC) is the application of the same 14 tools to control process *inputs* (independent variables). Figure 99 portrays these relationships.

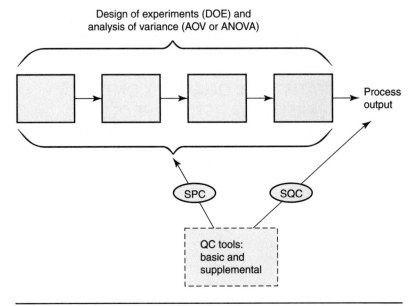

Figure 99 SQC versus SPC.

STRATEGIC PLANNING FOR QUALITY

Any organization that wants to thrive, not just survive, creates a strategic plan. Using whatever level of quantitative detail is necessary, this plan precisely describes what the organizational leadership has established as its annual goals for a specified time period, for example, three to five years hence. Strategic planning for quality should be considered to be a subject of policy deployment.

In addition, the plan denotes the type and extent of resources necessary to achieve the goals. As might be expected, this requires a number of resource trade-offs since few, if any, organizations have sufficient resources to accomplish all of their goals simultaneously.

It becomes necessary to specify evaluatory criteria, weighted according to the needs of the organization, as determined by the organizational leadership. While there are a number of ways to efficiently create a strategic plan, one of the most effective is the combined use of brainstorming, affinity analysis, the prioritization matrix, and Pareto analysis.

This approach ensures that hidden agendas are exposed, every goal is specifically addressed by one or more of the necessary and influential resources, and these resources are allocated according to the priorities of the goals, the availability and cost of the resources, and the extent to which each resource influences the capability of the organization to achieve each goal.

Some organizations have chosen to have a separate strategic plan for each major organizational function (finance, marketing, engineering, operations, quality). While this approach to strategic planning is superior to no planning at all, it is inferior to the creation of a strategic plan that contains an orchestrated description of what the organization wishes to accomplish and links the goals and resources of the entire enterprise together into a coordinated whole (see Figure 100).

The quality component of a strategic plan is that portion of the enterprisewide strategic plan that brings the quality function and its associated responsibilities in juxtaposition with those of the remainder of the organization. These various responsibilities, including quality engineering, inspection, supplier quality, and metrology, must be coordinated with their counterpart functions throughout the organization. This coordination is necessary to ensure that whatever resources may be required by the quality function are included in the enterprisewide resource allocation plan.

Strategic Planning for Quality

Each year, a five-year strategic plan is developed, using information from market analysis, competitive and industry data, and evolving technology. This plan describes the long-term business and quality goals set by the company.

Five-Year Strategic Plan

Customers are included in the strategic planning process, providing product direction, and suppliers assist in the product sourcing strategy. Teams of employees develop a business strategy that includes product and business goals. Manufacturing, development, marketing, service, and support teams develop functional strategies that contain the quality improvement plans required to achieve the business strategy. Functional strategies describe the resources, capital, and expenses required to achieve the quality priorities and the business strategy.

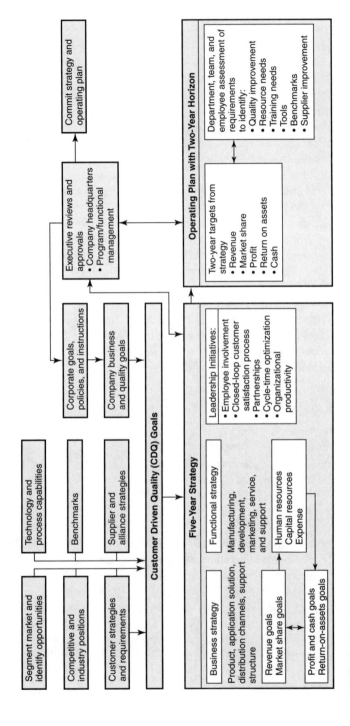

Figure 100 Strategic planning.

STRUCTURED INTERVIEW APPROACH

Since not all interviewing techniques will fit every possible situation, some general guidelines should be considered. A structured interview approach is composed of the following guidelines and should be used with care.

Before beginning an interview, prepare questions to be asked after an interviewee tells his or her story. Conduct the interview in a quiet, neutral, nonthreatening location, not one likely to be a source of intimidation.

Make certain the interviewee knows and understands the purpose of the interview. He or she may react more favorably to being questioned when told you are only trying to learn more about a specific event. The interviewee should not be misled about the purpose of the interview. Be sure to inform him or her fully and don't deviate from the stated purpose of the interview.

Get essential information on record: name, address, where the interviewee can be reached, and so on. It is best to do this prior to the start of the interview.

Let the interviewee tell the story in his or her terms, not yours. Let the event in question be described in whatever way he or she remembers it (what was seen, what was heard) and do not interrupt. Try starting with, "Tell me what you saw or did in the order it happened. Start with when you first became aware of the event."

Speak using the interviewee's terms, not yours. He or she may not know a lathe from a mill.

Encourage the interviewee to use models or sketches to help illustrate his or her story.

Use a recording device if it is possible to be unobtrusive. Explain why you are using the machine and gain approval by the interviewee. As he or she talks, make notes quietly and discreetly on questions you may want to ask later, particularly regarding those remarks that corroborate statements made by the interviewee or others.

If the interviewee doesn't know where to begin his or her story, a good lead is, "What first called your attention to the event?" This is likely to start the interviewee talking.

Avoid leading questions. You may pressure the interviewee to respond in a particular direction, and since he or she is often eager to please, the direction can easily be biased.

Tact, courtesy, and diplomacy are good rules for an interview. Be neutral but interested, friendly, courteous, and businesslike. Approach the interviewee as an equal. Urge him or her onward, but don't appear to be in a hurry. Seek cooperation.

At the conclusion of the interview, be sure to ask the interviewee if there is anything he or she would like to add that hasn't already been discussed.

SUPPLY CHAIN MANAGEMENT (SCM)

Supply chain management (SCM), also known as value chain management or supply and demand chain management, is in its broadest sense an understanding of the virtual enterprise. The scope extends from second-tier suppliers through production to customers and consumers. The process flowchart for SCM is portrayed in Figure 101.

Multiple methodologies and tools exist for improving supply chains. Whenever possible, they should be combined and used with cross-functional teams to attain additional leverage, that is, the reduction of cycle time and costs as well as optimization of the entire supply chain (see Figure 102).

Supply chain management is about attacking those time-sensitive activities that are not perceived by your customers as adding value. SCM is not about working harder; it is about working smarter (see Figure 103).

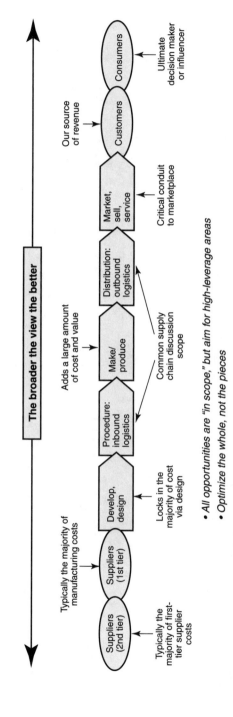

Figure 101   Supply chain management process flowchart.

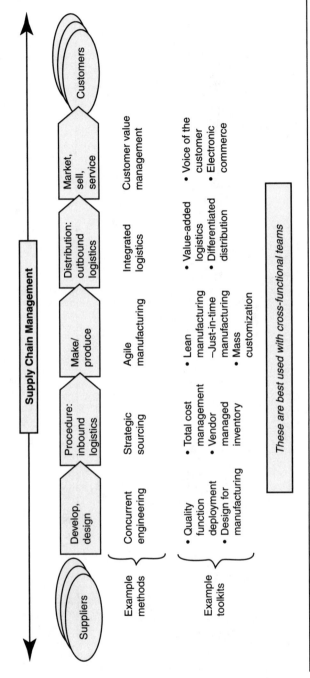

Figure 102 Supply chain management process improvement.

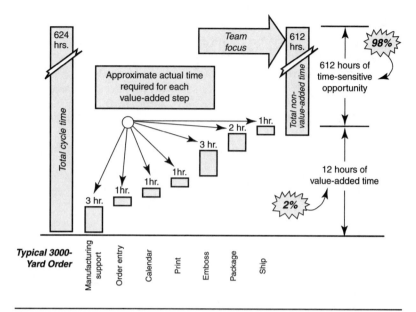

Figure 103   Supply chain management—process analysis.

SURVEY ANALYSIS

Survey analysis is an effective way to determine what customers, suppliers, team members, management/supervisors, and/or employees are thinking, both individually and collectively. This approach to collecting both quantitative and qualitative data provides information on what processes, functions, or areas need to be improved, and what needs to be done to achieve the improvements. In addition, the use of survey analysis provides insights regarding implementation of programs, projects, and initiatives.

Questions contained in the survey analysis can be either open-ended, closed-ended, or both. Open-ended questions are relatively easy to prepare, but require considerable expertise to interpret. They provide opportunities for respondents to communicate their thoughts without having to choose from a set of predetermined choices. Persons conducting the survey on behalf of its sponsor can use thematic content analysis to extract key points or issues from the collection of returned survey instruments or questionnaires.

Closed-ended questions are more difficult to prepare than open-ended questions but are quite easy to interpret. Because they are also easier to complete, more questions about more topics can be asked and completed in the same amount of time as a much shorter set of open-ended questions.

A word of caution: the longer it takes to respond to a survey, the lower the proportion that will be completed and returned. Thus, survey preparation is a trade-off between the number and type of questions asked, versus the proportion that can be expected to be returned.

Survey analysis also provides an understanding of what changes are occurring over time, that is, whether things are getting better or worse relative to the results obtained in an earlier, baseline survey. These are referred to as longitudinal changes.

Examples

Management Survey

How well do individuals in your department cooperate?

Minimal		Average		Maximum
1	2	3	4	5

How well do departments cooperate?

Minimal		Average		Maximum
1	2	3	4	5

Customer Survey

Does our product meet your needs?

Never	Sometimes	Always
1	2	3

Is our service timely?

Never	Sometimes	Always
1	2	3

SYNCHRONOUS WORKSHOP

A synchronous workshop is used to initiate, organize, and implement synchronous manufacturing. The workshop focuses on the improvement process necessary to optimize a facility's production output and to minimize the costs associated with its operation.

This is accomplished, insofar as is possible, by eliminating periods of idle time (including transportation, queuing, and inspection/ test time), reducing setup and processing time for each unit of production, and improving quality (by reducing defect rates and unit-to-unit variation).

A synchronous workshop is organized around the multiple concepts of synchronous manufacturing and the functional constraints that are unique to a specific organization, as follows:

Concepts of Synchronous Manufacturing

- Integrated product and process development (IPPD)
- Integration of material management with manufacturing
- Implementation of just-in-time inventory control
- Integrated manufacturing
- Implementation of standardized management systems for cost, personnel, facilities, and material

Specific Organizational Functional Constraints

- Marketplace
- Material availability
- Plant capacity
- Logistics
- Managerial
- Personnel
- Financial
- Product line

- Equipment

- Customers

- Suppliers

- Location

- Transportation

Once the goals and objectives for a synchronous workshop have been established, the focus should be on a single activity, facility, or product line. A high-level, cross-functional, multidisciplinary team is then empowered to achieve implementation of synchronous manufacturing. Once the team has been trained on the concepts of synchronous manufacturing, a very specific plan of action is developed by and for the team.

Specific dates, resources, facilities, and personnel in support of a concentrated effort by the entire team will be needed for the team to accomplish its work. The result of the team effort is its implementation plan and, subsequently, the managed execution of the plan.

SYSTEMS ANALYSIS

Systems analysis is a way of studying the interrelated entirety of an enterprise including the connections between functions. This is in contrast to functional analysis where the functions are considered without necessarily studying their effects on dependent functions. Without systems analysis, it is possible to optimize specific functions to the detriment of the entire system.

Systems analysis can pertain to many types of systems. Here, the emphasis is on the enterprise system that develops, produces, and delivers a tangible product and/or an intangible service. In this context, systems analysis addresses the flows of materials and services between functions as well as the information (signals) necessary to coordinate functional responsibilities. Systems analysis evaluates the adequacy of these flows as well as the measures of effectiveness (MOEs) and the technical performance measures (TPMs) necessary to evaluate the health of the system. These MOEs and TPMs are commonly referred to as performance measures/metrics.

Systems analysis can include the concept of performance measures/metrics allocation. An allocation is a target value for a function's performance. If all the functions of an enterprise perform up to their allocation, the overall system performance will be achieved, and vice versa.

Checklist or Implementation Steps*

1. Acquire and review all system documentation, system specifications, flowcharts, drawings, standards, parts lists, and customer requirements.

2. Acquire all available data from all sources for the system under study.

3. Prepare a system hardware schematic or flowchart if the system drawings are not descriptive enough to clearly demonstrate all component, subassembly, and assembly interfaces.

4. Prepare a system functional flow diagram describing the functional flow and sequences of operation of the system.

5. Utilize all the available data to quantify the elements of the functional flow.

6. Allocate the elements of the functional flow to specific components, subassemblies, and assemblies of the schematic.

7. Evaluate the resulting systems analysis for improvement opportunities for corrective action.

SYSTEMS ENGINEERING

Systems engineering is a management technology. For the sake of clarification, management involves interaction of an organization with its environment. In this context, environment is generally interpreted to include the total external milieu surrounding both individuals and their organizations. Technology involves the delivery by an organization of scientific applications for the intended improvement of humankind. Thus, systems engineering as a management technology involves scientific applications, organizations, and their environments.

---

* Not all of the listed steps pertain to each system.

The process of systems engineering involves working with customers, either internal or external to an organization, to assist them in the arrangement of knowledge in order to aid them in both judgment and selection activities. These activities result in the making of decisions and associated resource allocations through enhanced efficiency, effectiveness, equity, and explicability as a result of systems engineering efforts.

The outcome of a systems engineering study is a set of design, analysis, management, direction, and regulation activities relative to the planning, development, production, and operation of total systems. This maintains overall integrity and integration as they are related to performance and reliability.

Systems engineering is an appropriate combination of mathematical, behavioral, and managerial theories applied in a useful setting that is appropriate for the resolution of complex real world issues of large scale and scope. As such, it consists of the use of managerial, behavioral, and mathematical models to identify, structure, analyze, evaluate, and interpret generally incomplete, uncertain, imprecise, and otherwise imperfect information.

When associated with a value system, this information leads to knowledge to permit decisions that have been developed with maximum possible understanding of their impacts. A central problem of systems engineering is to select methods that are explicit and rational as well as compatible with the actual implementation framework and the perspectives and knowledge bases of those responsible for decision activities, such that decision making and the resulting policies become as efficient, effective, equitable, and explicable as possible.

Systems engineering practitioners make extensive use of many of the methods described in this book as well as a variety of complex methodologies that go well beyond its scope.

TALLY SHEET

A tally sheet provides a systematic method for collecting data. In most cases, it is a form designed to collect specific data (see Figure 104). This tool provides a consistent, effective, and economical approach to gathering data, organizing it for analysis, and displaying it for preliminary review.

A tally sheet can be used with either attribute or variable data. It sometimes takes the form of a manual data collection form where automated data is not necessary or available. It should be designed to minimize the need for complicated entries. Simple to understand, straightforward tally sheets are key to successful data gathering.

	Supplier				
Defect	**A**	**B**	**C**	**D**	**Total**
Incorrect invoice	////	/		//	7
Incorrect inventory	7///	//	/	/	9
Damaged material	///		//	///	8
Incorrect test documentation	/	///	////	//	10
Total	13	6	7	8	34

Figure 104 Sample tally sheet.

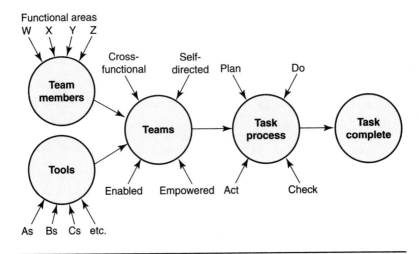

Figure 105 Teams, tools, and tasks.

TEAMS, TOOLS, AND TASKS

It isn't necessary to be a chemist to know that a fire cannot be started without a fuel and an oxidizer. But it must be pointed out that it takes the right fuel and a corresponding oxidizer to create the foundation for a really good fire.

Using a similar line of reasoning, it should be obvious that it takes the right team members equipped with the right tools to create an enabled, empowered, motivated, cross-functional, self-directed team capable of selecting the most important tasks, and then efficiently and effectively solving the most critical problems.

This concept is depicted in Figure 105.

THEMATIC CONTENT ANALYSIS (TCA)

Thematic content analysis (TCA) is a method for analyzing qualitative or communications data to determine patterns of thought. It is useful in survey analysis as well as in analysis of the results of interviews and focus groups.

Basically, TCA is the organization of nonquantitative data by common themes to determine the frequency with which the themes appear. This information can then be used to prioritize the data or determine courses of action. Other tools and techniques used in conjunction with TCA include affinity analysis, tally sheets, data tables, and Pareto analysis.

Checklist or Implementation Steps

1. Collect the data by surveys, questionnaires, or interviews.

2. Combine the answers for each question on separate lists. Each time an answer is repeated, place a tick mark beside the response. If there are responses that do not clearly fit in one of the categories, establish a miscellaneous category. If the miscellaneous category gradually becomes large, analyze it to determine if there are themes within it.

3. Total the responses by theme for each question and determine the recurring themes in the responses.

Thematic content analysis.

Frequency	Answers to Question #1	Major Themes
	a.	I
	b.	II
	c.	III
	d.	–
	–	–
	–	–
	–	–

TILMAG

TILMAG is a German acronym for a systematic and structured idea generation methodology developed by Dr. Helmut Schlicksupp in Germany during the 1970s:

Transformation

Idealer

Losungelemente in

Matrixen fur

Assoiciation und

Gemeinsamkeiten

Loosely translated, TILMAG means "the translation of ideal solution elements in a matrix for associations and things in common"

TILMAG has useful application when a team needs to find ingenious, creative materials from fields other than their own for application to an immediate problem or concern. TILMAG can also be used when a team cannot depend solely on word and picture association to help produce needed ideas.

TILMAG provides for guided or controlled associations that are captured in a special matrix referred to as an association matrix. This matrix allows associations to become further developed.

TILMAG is performed in three phases: creating a list of ideal solution elements, generating optimum associations, and applying analogous principles back to a problem. Each phase can be completed by the same team or by separate teams. This feature provides additional flexibility with respect to either time or special skills of the participants who need to be involved.

TIME STUDY ANALYSIS

Time study analysis is a technique for establishing a time standard for the performance of a specific task. Time studies can be useful for predicting labor costs and process cycle times.

This technique uses measurements of work content of a task performed in a specified manner. Time studies include allowances for fatigue as well as personal and unavoidable delays. A time study uses sampling to assure accurate estimates of work content.

Time study analysis is performed for the most part by industrial engineers using either manual or computerized data collection and analysis techniques.

TOTAL QUALITY MANAGEMENT VERSUS CONTINUOUS IMPROVEMENT (TQM VERSUS CI)

Total Quality Management

Total quality management (TQM) is an evolving management philosophy and methodology for guiding the continuous improvement (CI) of products, services, and processes with the objective of realizing optimum customer value and satisfaction.

Continuous Improvement

Continuous improvement (CI) is a disciplined process for understanding, analyzing, and continually improving organizational work processes, capabilities, and procedures with the objective of meeting or exceeding customer expectations. The following are some of the characteristics of CI:

- Every work process has a variety of undiscovered improvement opportunities waiting to be realized.

- The use of structured methods using graphic techniques for analysis, measurement, and decision support leads to better improvement solutions than does the use of unstructured methodologies.

- Consistently meeting or exceeding customer expectations can best be achieved by people working together on teams to improve their work processes.

- The improvement of the quality of an organization's products, services, and processes inevitably leads to improved productivity and profits.

Are TQM and CI Different Acronyms for the Same Process?

Some say yes and others say no. Both opinions are presented here:

- Many organizations use the terms interchangeably.

- Some organizations start to implement TQM by implementing CI projects.

- CI, directed at achieving improved quality and customer satisfaction, is a strategy for achieving the goals of TQM.

- TQM is a philosophy and methodology that significantly differs from traditional command and control management.

- CI can be implemented with some benefit in a traditionally managed organization. Thus, CI is not the same as TQM.

- CI is just one of the aspects that an organization requires for a TQM program.

TREE DIAGRAM

The tree diagram has many applications in the TQM/CI/Six Sigma arena because it is a systematic tool for determining all the tasks necessary to accomplish a specific goal. It can be used for determining the key factors that are the source of a particular problem or for creating a fully developed action plan for a single event or a process. The tree diagram can also be used to decide on the priority for a given action (see Figures 106 and 107).

This tool uses linear logic to move from a broad statement to successive levels of detail. The statement can be generated using affinity analysis, an interrelationship digraph, or brainstorming.

The tree diagram is quite useful, therefore, when a task or problem is complex and when it is important to identify all the key elements or subtasks of which the task or problem is composed.

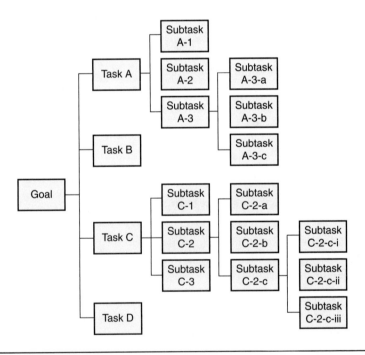

Figure 106 Tree diagram—example 1.

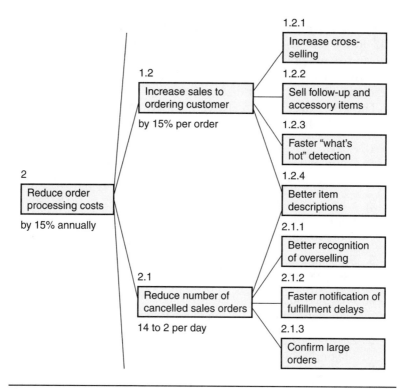

Figure 107 Tree diagram—example 2.

TRIZ (TIPS)

TRIZ (pronounced treez) is a Russian acronym for a unique methodology for increasing engineering innovation and radically improving engineering design. In the United States and Europe, TRIZ is also referred to as the *theory of innovative problem solving* (TIPS) or *systematic innovation*.

Whatever this latest and greatest approach to problem solving and engineering innovation is called, it is a powerful tool that eliminates the need for compromise and trade-offs caused by conflicts or dysfunctional relationships between performance characteristics.

Russian Genrich Altshuller (1926–2003) developed the basis of TRIZ in the late 1940s by examining and classifying thousands of Russian patent applications. This resulted in his defining five levels of creativity, more than 80 technical and physical contradictions, and numerous other important discoveries.

The five levels of creativity (degrees of inventiveness) as defined by Altshuller are:

1. *Apparent or conventional solution: 32 percent*
   Solution accomplished by methods well known within a specialty

2. *Small invention inside of paradigm: 45 percent*
   Improvement of an existing system, usually with some compromise

3. *Substantial invention inside technology: 18 percent*
   Essential improvement of existing system

4. *Invention outside technology: 4 percent*
   New generation of design using science not technology

5. *Discovery: 1 percent*
   Major discovery and new science

Altshuller believed that knowledge about many inventions should be extracted, compiled, and generalized to enable easy access by inventors in all areas. Clearly, those persons who are charged with the responsibility for inventing, or are personally driven to invent, better, faster, and cheaper solutions to chemical, mechanical, electrical, nuclear, and other problems should learn as much as they can about TRIZ or TIPS. Without this knowledge, they are putting themselves, their patrons, their employers, and/or their professional associates at a significant disadvantage.

VALUE ENGINEERING (VE)

Value engineering (VE) is a discipline that emphasizes the removal of all unnecessary costs from the design of a product, service, or process. VE teams develop cost-effective alternatives to original designs while retaining or enhancing customer requirements. This is accomplished by conducting a comprehensive design review and structured VE analysis.

Products, like processes, begin with or evolve features or functions that later prove unnecessary. Value engineering is similar in purpose and procedure to business process reengineering in that it takes a fresh look at the original design to enhance the function while reducing unnecessary elements and costs.

Other tools used in association with VE include brainstorming, the Gantt chart, and the interrelationship digraph.

VARIABILITY REDUCTION
PROCESS (VRP)

Dr. W. Edwards Deming, perhaps the best-known advocate of quality and continuous improvement, said, "If I had to reduce my message to a few words, I'd say it's to reduce variation."

This is strong stuff coming from the man who helped save Japan in the 1950s and then helped turn around American industry in the 1980s. Why did he select the variability reduction process (VRP) as the focal point of his lifelong mission? The simple answer is because of the critical importance of making the outputs of processes more predictable, uniform, and consistent, and as a direct consequence, more dependable.

No two people are exactly alike, even identical twins. That's fine for people; it's great to be unique. Unfortunately, no two products are exactly alike either. This can become a real problem. Imagine having to replace a failed part in your car. After making a trip or two to an auto parts store and then working on the car for an hour or more, you realize that the replacement is not the same as the failed part even though it's precisely the same part number. By now you're really frustrated. When you expect a part, a paint color, or a wallpaper pattern to be identical to it's counterpart, it can drive you nuts if it isn't.

It is this sort of variability that needs to be reduced and, insofar as is possible, eliminated. The more a process output varies from one unit to another, the less able an organization is to predict how well the unit will meet its specs and, ultimately, satisfy its customers. If it can't be predicted, it can't be controlled. When it can't be controlled, it is going to cause customer frustration and dissatisfaction but perhaps not for too much longer.

If you play golf or any other sport, one of the primary goals is to become consistent. The objective in golf is to put the ball in the cup in as few shots as possible. Every golf course and each of its holes has a par, the expected number of shots or strokes it should take. If you usually score in the 90s, and then one day you record a par game, you really shouldn't leave your current position with the intent of becoming the local pro.

When you have consistency in your game, you regularly and systematically improve your score by reducing the number of strokes (defects) you require to complete a game. If your game is erratic, ranging from a rare par game to a dreadful round in the 120s, chances are that you aren't learning from your play. The process improvement strategy an organization should pursue is a systematic approach to gaining control over variability with the strategic goal of variability reduction.

Figure 108 illustrates how a continuous measurable improvement initiative can be supported by the VRP concept. With respect to Figure 109 having listened to the voice of the customer, QFD is used to prioritize where improvements are needed. Then, DOE (robust design) is applied to provide the mechanism necessary for identifying these improvements. Finally, SPC contributes the means

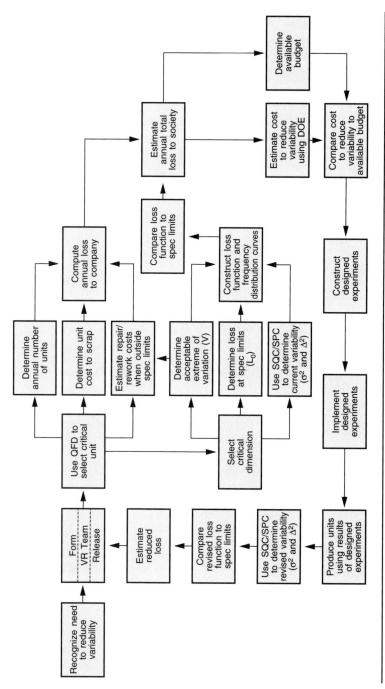

Figure 108 Continuous measurable improvement using the variability reduction process.

to hold these gains as well as to otherwise ensure continuous improvement (kaizen).

Whether you're in a hospital clinic, a manufacturing area, or using a vise in a workshop, putting the squeeze on variation should be at the top of your "to do" list. Refer to Figure 110.

Variability Reduction Process

Customer	Quality function deployment (QFD)	Design of experiments (DOE)	Statistical process control (SPC)	Product

Knowledge feedback

Identify needs	Identify important items	Make improvements	Hold gains	Provide satisfaction

Figure 109 Variability reduction process.

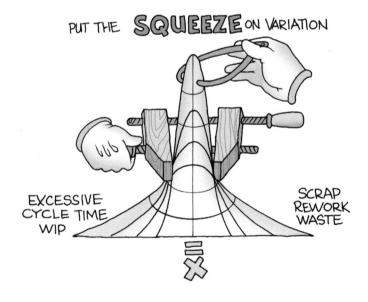

PUT THE **SQUEEZE** ON VARIATION

EXCESSIVE CYCLE TIME WIP

SCRAP REWORK WASTE

Figure 110 Squeezing variation.

VOICE OF THE CUSTOMER TABLE (VOCT)

The Kano model and the voice of the customer table (VOCT) are used at the front end of quality function deployment (QFD). Together they provide the means to listen to and better understand customers making use of products or services. Thus, it is possible to learn how they are used and then apply organizational capabilities to these products and services based on the spoken and unspoken needs of the customer.

The pursuit of customer satisfaction is more urgent when competitors catch up and are poised to surpass your company. The design and development time available to deliver newer and more exciting products and services to the market is shrinking, making it more difficult than ever for companies to stay ahead of the competition. QFD gives you an edge, but remember, competitors are using it too.

The VOCT gives an added edge to users of QFD. It is a two-part tool used to provide structure and a process for seeking out those items that the customer *wants*. It is also employed to reveal other items that they may not yet be aware of to achieve early discovery of the customer's true needs (see Figure 111).

In Part I of the VOCT, data are gathered about how the product or service is being used or could be used by the customer. These data come from interviews, questionnaires, observation of the customer's process in action, or an interrelationship digraph of the customer's use.

In Part II of the VOCT, the voice of the customer is reworded into customer demands taking into account all of the uses described in Part I. Demands take on many forms such as demands for quality, performance, low price, long life, safety, and low environmental impact. The QFD design team must interpret these various demands from the voice of the customer, the usage, and the operating environment. After the demands have been extrapolated from the VOCT, the demands are sorted to make later prioritization more effective.

QFD projects that have used the VOCT have found good results. While use of the VOCT adds an additional step to the design and development process, it provides a structure for team members in which to work together analyzing customer data. It makes the resulting QFD matrices smaller, better organized, and easier to work with. Some teams have said that their VOCT phase was the most valuable part of QFD.

Voice of the Customer	Use					
	Who	**What**	**When**	**Where**	**Why**	**How**
Easy to find during nighttime power failure	Adults; kids	See during power failure	Night	House; basement	See in dark; check circuit	Hold in hand; set on surface

VOCT—Part I for a flashlight

Reworded Demands	Demanded Quality	Quality Characteristics	Function	Reliability	Other
Can hold easily	Can hold easily				
Can use hands-free	Can use hands-free				
Maintain aiming			Maintain aiming		
Fits in drawer		Diameter			
Always ready to use				Does not work	

VOCT—Part II for a flashlight

Reworded Demands	Demanded Quality	Quality Characteristics	Function	Reliability	Other
Can hold easily	Can hold easily				
Can use hands-free	Can use hands-free				
Maintain aiming	Can see easily ←		Maintain aiming		
Fits in drawer	Can store easily ←	Size			
Always ready to use				Does not work	

Analyzing and organizing demands

Figure 111 Voice of the customer table example.

WORD–PICTURE ASSOCIATION

When a team stays within the traditional boundaries of a problem-solving process, it will find traditional solutions. It is unlikely that these solutions will be new, novel, or creative. By slightly shifting or redefining a problem, more creative materials can be generated for application to the original problem. (See *imaginary brainstorming*.)

Going a step further, the use of word–picture association results in "thinking outside the box." When different fields are explored, the result is a collection of worthwhile ideas and concepts that become available for application to an immediate problem or concern.

Word–picture association is a technique designed to assist in the generation of new ideas through the connection of pictures, words, or inventions. A team can study some projected photos or images and then be queried regarding what ideas were stimulated. Random words derived from lists or even dictionaries can be used to initiate ideas for application to a particular problem or concern. These words, images, and concepts can be used to stimulate ideas by simple analogy from inventions that share principles similar to the problem or concern being studied.

The mechanisms of word–picture association push its users outside the immediate field of the problem and make it possible to search for new ideas by involving as many other fields as possible.

There are four target tools used as a part of this technique: stimulating word analysis, catalogue technique, picture projection, and bio-techniques. There are two systematically planned paths designed for using these tools: analogous thinking (for analogies) and random search methods (for stimulating terms and associations).

Z

Z-SCORE

If a normal distribution has a mean (μ) of zero and a standard deviation (σ) of 1.0, it is referred to as the standard normal distribution. When this is the case, areas under any normal frequency distribution curve can be obtained by performing a change in scale (see Figure 112). This change of scale converts the units of measurement from the original (or x) scale into standard units, standard scores, or z-scores, by means of the formula:

$$z = \frac{x - \mu}{\sigma}$$

In this new z-scale, the value of z (the z-score), is the number of standard deviations the corresponding value of x lies above or below the mean of its distribution. Knowing the value of z allows you to determine the area under the normal curve from one point on the x scale to another. Because of the unique properties of the normal distribution, that is, the mean, median, and mode having equal values, the area under the curve between any two values of x is equal to the probability of this event taking place.

The concept of the z-score has been advanced to include special cases of z. For example, Z_U is a dimensionless index used to measure the location of a process, that is, its central tendency, relative to its standard deviation and the process upper specification limit (USL). If the process frequency distribution is normal, the value of Z_U can be used to determine the percentage of the area located above the USL.

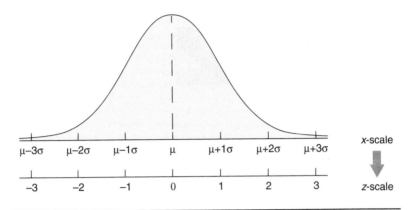

Figure 112   Change of scale to standard units.

Z_L is also a dimensionless index used to measure the location of a process, that is, its central tendency, relative to its standard deviation and the process lower specification limit (LSL). If the process frequency distribution is normal, the value of Z_L can be used to determine the percentage of the area below the LSL.

Z_{MIN} results from a comparison of the Z_U and Z_L values and is the smaller of the two. It is used to calculate C_{PK}, the mean-sensitive process capability index.

Z-SERIES MATRICES

The Z-series, created by Richard Zultner in the late 1980s, is composed of three matrices.

They are used to supplement the 30-matrix approach to quality function deployment (QFD) used by GOAL/QPC and the four-matrix approach to QFD used by the American Supplier Institute (ASI). While the GOAL/QPC and ASI approaches are used for traditional QFD projects on products and services, the Z-series matrices are used in conjunction with software quality deployment.

The Z-series are composed of the Z0, Z1, and Z2 matrices. The Z0 matrix deals with the identification and organization of potential software users. The Z1 matrix is used to refine user expressions of need into statements of user expectations. The Z2 matrix maps entities against processes to ensure that the process and data models represented on an entity/interrelationship digraph are mutually consistent.

Glossary

The following terms are used in the fields of Six Sigma, TQM, continuous improvement, quality improvement, quality assurance, and quality control. They are included here as quick reference material.

3 Ps (Purpose/Process/Payoff)—Key areas to discuss at the start of a meeting or presentation are the purpose of the meeting, the process that will be followed, and the payoff to the group.

5Ms & 1E (Men/Women, Method, Machine, Measurement, Material, and Environment)—The possible causes in a cause-and-effect analysis, as well as the independent variable inputs to a process that affect the dependent variable output.

5S Method—Notation for the 5S activities that make any workplace cleaner and safer as well as every job simpler and more satisfying. It's about how to create a workplace that is visibly organized, free of clutter, arranged so things can be found, and sparkling clean. In English: *sort, set* in order, *shine, standardize* and *sustain.* In Japanese: *seiri, seiton, seiso, seiketsu,* and *shitsuke.*

5Ws & 1H (Who, What, Where, When, Why and How)—A useful tool to help develop an objective and a concise statement of the problem.

acceptance sampling—Evaluating a portion of a product lot for the purpose of accepting or rejecting the entire lot as either conforming or not conforming to a quality specification.

action plan—The steps a team develops to implement a solution or the actions needed to make continued progress toward a solution.

activities—Segments of programs that, when coordinated, add up to a particular program.

adaptable process—A process capable of being changed to accommodate future business requirements.

AOQ (average outgoing quality)—The expected quality of outgoing product following the use of an acceptance sampling plan for a given value of incoming product quality.

AOQL—For a given acceptance sampling plan, the maximum AOQ over all possible levels of incoming quality.

array (of numbers)—A data set arranged in order from greatest to least value or vice versa.

assignable cause—The name for the source of variability in a process that is not due to chance and therefore can be identified and eliminated. (See *special cause*.)

attributes (discrete) data—Data obtained by counting either nonconforming items or the occurrences of nonconformities.

benchmaking—The search for the best practices leading to the superior performance of an organization.

Black Belt—A Six Sigma organizational role that requires exceptional management, leadership, and technical skills and calls for careful selection and training. Black Belts lead process improvement teams (PITs) and train Green Belts.

brainstorming—An idea-generating technique that uses group interaction to generate many ideas in a short time period.

breakthrough—A change: a dynamic, decisive movement to new, higher levels of performance. Used by J. M. Juran to describe a new, improved level of sustained quality performance.

$\bar{c}$—The center (average) line of a c-chart.

cause—A proven reason for the existence of one or more defects.

cause-and-effect diagram—A structured form of brainstorming that graphically shows the relationship of causes and subcauses to an identified effect (problem). (See *fishbone diagram* or *Ishikawa diagram*.)

c-chart—An attribute control chart used when n (subgroup size) is constant to evaluate the number of defects (nonconformances) per subgroup. Because the c-chart is based on the Poisson distribution, $\bar{c}$, (the centerline) is equal to the population variance.

Champion (Sponsor)—A Six Sigma organizational role for a senior manager who monitors the work of a process improvement team (PIT). Insures that his or her PIT projects are aligned with organizational priorities as well as setting and maintaining broad goals for improvement projects. Removes barriers and makes resources available for PITs.

chance cause—The name for the source of variability in a process that occurs randomly. (See *common cause*.)

charter—A commitment by management in document form stating the scope of authority for an improvement group.

check sheet—A tool for gathering information about a problem and its probable causes by collecting and organizing two or more kinds of information at the same time.

checklist—A sequential list of items to be attended to or of steps to be taken.

chronic problem—A long-standing adverse situation that requires solution by changing either the process or the status quo.

class—A quantitatively defined subgroup of an entire range of data.

class interval—The width or size of each class in a histogram, each of which must be the same to ensure accurate results.

class limits—Those quantitative values that actually separate class intervals. Class limits must be set so none of the values occurring in the data set can fall on any class limit.

code of cooperation—A list of actions or behaviors agreed to by the team that fosters cooperative team interactions and effective team decisions.

common cause—A cause of variation in a process that is random and uncontrollable. (See *chance cause*.)

confidence level—The probability that an interval about a sample statistic (such as the mean) actually includes the comparable population parameter.

confidence limits—The end points of the interval about the sample statistic that is believed, with a specified confidence level, to include the population parameter.

consensus decision—A decision made after all aspects of an issue, both positive and negative, have been brought out to the extent that everyone openly understands and supports the decision and the reasons for making it.

continuous (variable) data—Data generated by measuring against a standard, for example, length using a ruler or tape measure, time using a stop watch, clock or calendar, or weight using a scale.

continuous improvement—Continuously monitoring processes to determine if they function as desired and if they can be improved.

control chart—A chart showing sequential or time-related performance of a process that is used to determine when the process is operating in or out of statistical control, using control limits defined on the chart.

control limits—A statistically derived limit for a process that indicates the spread of variation attributable to chance variation in the process. Control limits are based on averages.

controllability study—A study to learn if defects are operator controllable or management controllable.

Conway, William E.—Incorporated the quality improvement process in Nashua Corporation as president and CEO. Developed "The Right Way to Manage" seminar.

cost of quality—The cost of conformance (achieving quality) plus the cost of nonconformance (waste).

C_P (process capability index)—A performance metric that quantitatively describes the ability of a centered process to deliver product within the design specification limits.

C_{PK} (mean-sensitive process capability index)—A performance metric that quantitatively describes the location of a process, whether centered or not, with respect to the design specification limits.

critical dependencies—The interrelationships existing within or among processes that are primary drivers of defects or errors in a product or service.

critical success factors—Indicators developed by a customer that point out the defect-free character of a product or service.

Crosby, Philip—Emphasized measuring quality in financial terms and created the concept of *zero defects.*

CTM (cycle time management)—A strategically oriented process used to reduce cycle time, thus increasing productivity and profits.

customer—Anyone for whom an organization provides goods or services; can be either internal or external.

cycle time—A performance metric composed of both essential and nonessential activities that quantitatively describes the duration of a complete cycle of a specified process or subprocess; does not include buffers.

defect—A nonconforming attribute.

defective—A unit with at least one nonconforming attribute.

degrees of freedom—A statistical measure that, in general, is the number of independent comparisons available to estimate a specific parameter and that serves as a means of entering certain statistical tables.

Deming, Dr. W. Edwards—Father of the "third wave" of the industrial revolution in Japan, who advocated quality and productivity improvement through SQC.

Deming wheel—Plan–do–check–act (PDCA). To achieve quality improvement, Dr. W. E. Deming said you must plan for it, implement it (do), analyze the results (check), and take action (act) for continuous improvement.

department task analysis—A method for analyzing an organization by determining its mission and how it interacts with customers and suppliers. Used to position the organization for improvement.

dependent variable—Its value (order of magnitude) depends on the value of one or more associated independent variables. (A person's weight is a dependent variable and is related to independent variables such as the person's height, caloric intake, metabolism, and so on.)

diagnosis—The process of studying symptoms, collecting and analyzing data, conducting experiments to test theories, and establishing relationships between causes and effects.

diagnostic arm—Term used by Juran to refer to a person or persons brought together to support data gathering and problem analysis.

discrete (attribute) data—Data generated by counting the frequency of occurrence of specific characteristics or events (number of defects, number of defectives, or number of late arrivals).

DOE (design of experiments)—Application of a collection of highly efficient and economical methods used together to reach valid and relevant conclusions.

DPMO (defects per million opportunities)—A performance metric used to identify the status of a process output. A 3.4 dpmo corresponds to a Six Sigma level of quality. (See *ppm*.)

effect—An observable action or evidence of a problem, that is, a dependent variable.

effective—A process that delivers a defect-free product or service to the customer.

efficient—A process that operates effectively while consuming the minimum amount of resources (labor, time, and so on).

errors, inadvertent—Worker errors that are unintentional, unwitting, and unpredictable.

errors, technique—Errors that arise because workers lack an essential technique, skill, or knowledge needed to avoid making the error.

errors, willful—Errors that workers know they are making.

events log—A detailed chronological listing of those process-related events that differ from the norm (with respect to men/women, material, methods, machines, measurements, and environment). Used in conjunction with process improvement centers (PICs).

facilitator—A person who functions as the coach or consultant to a group, team, or organization. In quality improvement, the facilitator focuses on process while the team leader focuses on content.

failure, accidental—Failure arising from misuse while in service.

failure, infant mortality—Early service life failure due to misapplication, design weaknesses, manufacturing mistakes, or shipping damage.

failure, wear out—Failure after acceptable service life.

fishbone diagram—Another name for a cause-and-effect diagram, which resembles a fish skeleton. Also called an Ishikawa diagram after the Japanese engineer who developed it. (See *cause-and-effect diagram*.)

fitness for use—The condition of goods and services that meet the needs of people who use them. Also, Dr. Juran's definition of *quality*.

flowchart—A chart that symbolically shows the input from suppliers, the sequential work activities, and the output to the customer.

force-field analysis—A list identifying promoting and inhibiting factors (forces) that must be overcome before opportunity or problem lists can be built or effective solutions can be implemented.

gatekeepers—Individuals who help others enter into a discussion (gate openers) and those who cut off others or interrupt them (gate closers).

goal—A statement describing a desired future condition or change, without being specific about how much and when.

Green Belt—A Six Sigma role associated with process stakeholders and other process improvement team (PIT) members. Requires fewer skills and less experience than a Black Belt.

histogram—A specific form of bar chart that illustrates the frequency distribution of a series of measurements of continuous (variable) data.

house of quality—The initial quality function deployment (QFD) matrix composed of the *whats*, the *hows*, a relationship matrix, an interaction matrix (the roof), and other "rooms."

hows—The organizational response variable in the QFD house of quality (substitute quality characteristics).

hugging—Occurs when more of the points on a control chart fall closer to the centerline or the control limit lines than would be expected by chance.

imagineering—Visualizing what a process without waste would look like as a goal for improvement activities.

impact changeability analysis—A tool for prioritizing a list of problems or opportunities by ranking them according to the degree of impact versus the ease of change.

implementers—Those individuals responsible for performing tasks within a process.

in control—A process operating without assignable causes of variation (special causes) is said to be *in a state of statistical control,* which is usually shortened to *in control.*

independent variable—Its value (order of magnitude) affects the value of an associated dependent variable. (See *dependent variable.*)

interaction matrix—The "roof" of the quality function deployment (QFD) house of quality located immediately above the *hows.* Used to establish the positive and negative influence each *how* has on all the other *hows.*

intervention—The role of a team facilitator when he or she interrupts a group to state observations about the group dynamics.

Ishikawa diagram—A name for a cause-and-effect diagram named after Dr. Kaoru Ishikawa, its developer. (See *cause-and-effect diagram* and *fishbone diagram.*)

JIT (just-in-time) training—Training provided to members of process improvement teams (PITs) just before a necessary tool and/or skill is needed for application.

Juran, Dr. Joseph—Emphasizes management's role in quality improvement by solving chronic problems, project by project.

just-in-time (JIT) inventory—The minimum inventory required to meet production schedules.

management-controllable defect—A defect that does not meet all of the criteria for an operator-controllable defect. (See *operator-controllable defect.*)

matrix concept—A group of elements with rows and columns designed to cross-reference multiple measurements or sets of data.

measurement—The dimension, quantity, or capacity determined by measuring against a standard reference.

meeting assessment—A process where the team collects information about the effectiveness of their meeting. (See *process check.*)

mission—The single overriding goal statement for an organization. It should encompass all organized activities that are significant in terms of resources used.

muda—A Japanese term meaning waste, specifically any human activity that absorbs resources but does not create value.

multivoting—A structured series of votes by a team that reduces a list containing a large number of items to a manageable few.

n—Notation for a sample size. (See *sample size.*)

N—Notation for a population size.

natural process limits—A three standard deviation (three sigma) spread, both above and below the mean of a process frequency distribution of individual occurrences. The natural process limits are not related to the specification limits but do reveal the extent of the process random variation.

NGT (nominal group technique)—A technique for generating a large number of ideas in a short period of time. NGT differs from brainstorming in that team members are asked to prepare a list of ideas prior to the session.

normal distribution—A continuous, symmetrical, bell-shaped frequency distribution of variables data.

$n\bar{p}$—The center (average) line of an $n\bar{p}$-chart.

$n\bar{p}$-chart—An attribute control chart used when n (subgroup size) is constant to evaluate the number of defective (nonconforming) units found in an inspection (or a series of inspections). The centerline of the $n\bar{p}$-chart is $n\bar{p}$.

number defective—Total number of defective units found in a sample.

number of defects—Total number of defects found in a sample.

objective—A more specific statement of the desired future condition or change than a goal. It includes measurable end results to be accomplished within specified time limits.

operational definition—A way to define something in observable or measurable terms.

operator-controllable defect—A defect that occurs where it is possible for operators to meet quality standards. It is controllable when operators know what is expected, know what their actual performance is, and have a means for regulation.

out of control—A process with variation outside the natural process limits.

owner—A manager assigned responsibility for the quality improvement of a process and given authority to make improvement happen.

$\bar{p}$—The center (average) line of a p-chart.

Pareto diagram—A bar chart prioritized in descending order from the left to right, distinguished by a cumulative percentage line that identifies the critical few opportunities for improvement.

p-chart—An attribute control chart used when n (subgroup size) is not constant to evaluate the fraction defective as nonconforming to specifications. The fraction defective, p, is defined as the ratio of the number of defective (nonconforming) units found in an inspection (or series of inspections) to the total number of units actually inspected. The centerline of the p-chart is $\bar{p}$.

PIC (process improvement center)—Usually a cork-faced bulletin board posted in proximity to its process. Contains printed documents that provide current process status including variable control charts and histograms (for variable data), attribute control charts and Pareto diagrams (for attribute data), process flowchart or process map, events log, and related general information (sample size, sampling rate, or defect data sheet).

PIT (process improvement team)—A collection of trained persons with a designated leader whose sole reason for coming together is to improve a specific process by reducing cycle time duration, cycle time variation, costs, and/or defects while simultaneously increasing customer satisfaction, profitability, and competitiveness.

ppm (parts per million)—A performance metric used to identify the status of a process output. A defect rate of 3.4 ppm corresponds to a Six Sigma level of quality. (See *dpmo*.)

problem statement—A statement that describes a problem and its impact in specific, concrete, and measurable terms.

process—A series of sequential, logically related, repeatable tasks that use organizational resources to provide a product or service to internal or external customers.

process analysis—Identification of specific, assignable causes of variation of a process quality characteristic.

process capability analysis—A statistical technique used during development and production cycles to analyze the variability of a process relative to product specifications.

process check—An assessment of the meeting process (versus content).

process flowchart—(See *flowchart.*)

process improvement—A comprehensive, well-defined method that describes and analyzes an organization's processes and sets the stage for effectively monitoring, improving, and controlling these processes.

process rating—The result of evaluating a process against criteria relating to its effectiveness, efficiency, and adaptability. The rating of a given process is improved through application of process improvement and assessed using ppm/dpmo, C_P/C_{PK}, or z-scale (sigma level).

program—A planned, organized effort directed at accomplishing an objective. A program specifies how an objective is to be reached.

PSP (problem-solving process)—A flowchart of specific tasks by which chronic system problems can be solved.

QFD (quality function deployment)—Translated from the Japanese, *hin-shitsu ki-no ten-kai,* QFD is a planning process that employs an interrelated set of matrices to collect and deploy the characteristics of a product or service desired by the customer throughout all the appropriate functional components of an organization to convert these customer inputs into technical specifics that can be acted upon by the organization.

quality—Consistently providing customers with products and services that meet their needs and expectations.

quality assurance—A collection of planned and systematic actions necessary to provide the desired confidence that a product or service will satisfy particular requirements.

quality audit—An independent evaluation of various aspects of quality performance.

quality circle—A group of people from the same work group who focus attention on ideas for improving quality within their own area. A quality initiative that preceded TQM.

quality control—The process of measuring quality performance, comparing it with a specific standard, and acting on the difference.

quality costs—(See *cost of quality*.)

quality improvement—A systematic method for improving processes to better meet customer needs and expectations.

quality improvement experts—(See *Conway, Crosby, Deming, Ishikawa, Juran,* and *Taguchi*.)

quality improvement team—A group of people who meet to identify, analyze, and solve chronic system problems or opportunities.

quality planning—Launching new products, processes, and so on, in which continuous improvement is built in.

r—Notation for the correlation coefficient of a *sample.* A number between –1 and +1 that indicates the degree of linear relationship that exists between two sets of numbers.

R—Notation for the range: the quantitative difference between the largest and smallest values in a data set.

R-chart—A control chart of the range of variable data as a function of time, lot number, or similar chronological variable.

random cause—(See *common cause* or *chance cause*.)

random sample—The number of units chosen from a lot by a method that gives each unit an equal chance of being selected.

randomization—A procedure for sample selection used to minimize risk associated with biases due to undetected or uncontrollable causes within inspections and experiments.

recorder—The person who takes minutes for meetings. (See *scribe*.)

relationship matrix—The center of the quality function deployment (QFD) house of quality with the *whats* on the left side and the *hows* across the top. Used to establish the extent of influence each *how* exercises in achieving each *what*.

remedy—See *solution*.

rework—To correct defects a process has produced.

root cause—The basic reason creating an undesired condition or problem. In many cases, the root cause may consist of several smaller causes.

run—The state of data plotted on a control chart in which points occur continually on one side of the centerline. The number of points is called the *length of the run*.

run chart—A graphic plot of a measurable characteristic of a process versus time.

s—Notation for the standard deviation of a sample.

$s_{\bar{x}}$—Notation for the standard error of the mean, the standard deviation of a sampling distribution.

sample size—Number of units (n) to be selected as random samples.

sampling—The taking of a group of units, portion of material, or observations from a larger collection of units, quantity of material, or observations that serves to provide information used as the basis for making a decision concerning the larger quantity.

sampling error—When less than 100 percent of a population is used to make a decision, any or all of three types of sampling error can occur: bias (lack of accuracy), dispersion (lack of precision), and nonreproducibility (lack of consistency).

scrap—The loss in labor and materials resulting from defects that cannot economically be repaired or used.

scribe—A person who writes inputs from a team on a pad or board. (See *recorder*.)

Six Sigma—A goal of near perfection (3.4 dpmo/ppm) in meeting customer requirements that demands an organizational culture change focusing on greater customer satisfaction, profitability, and competitiveness. Its highly skilled, well-trained practiners use a full range of process improvement tools to simultaneously increase quality, reduce cycle time, and strengthen customer loyalty.

SME (subject matter expert)—A person with specialized and extensive knowledge about a particular process, product, or service. An SME may or may not be included as a member of a process improvement team (PIT) depending upon the extent of his or her involvement.

solution—An intervention or corrective action which, when introduced, is expected to successfully eliminate (neutralize) or at least reduce a dysfunctional independent variable (cause of defects).

SPC (statistical process control)—Application of statistical tools (such as control charts, histograms, Pareto diagrams, scatter diagrams) to analyze the status of process *inputs* so as to take necessary and appropriate actions to achieve and maintain a state of statistical control of the process *outputs*. SPC locates and displays variation in a process to identify special/ assignable causes.

special cause—A cause of variation in a process that is not random or an uncontrollable cause. (In contrast to a *common cause*.)

specification limits—Limits established for a process output that are determined by engineering, development, management, or the customer. Specification limits are applied to individual occurrences and are directly related to natural process limits.

sporadic problem—A sudden adverse change in status quo requiring a solution that returns the condition to the original state.

SQC (statistical quality control)—Application of statistical tools (such as control charts, histograms, Pareto diagrams, scatter diagrams) to analyze the status of process *outputs* so as to take necessary and appropriate actions to achieve and maintain a state of statistical control of the process *inputs*. SQC locates and displays variation in a process to identify special/assignable causes.

stable process—A process in statistical control.

standard deviation—A mathematical term expressing the variability in a data set or process.

steering arm—Term used by Dr. Joseph Juran that refers to a person or persons from various departments who give direction and advice on an improvement program.

STP (situation, target, potential solution) analysis—A method to organize information (perceptions) about a problem into three categories: the way things are now (situation), what the group wants to accomplish (target), and information about ways to get from the current situation to the desired target or outcome (potential solution).

stratification—Division of a group into two or more subgroups on the basis of certain factors, for example, people can be stratified by gender, age, race, religion, education, and/or income.

structure tree diagram—A visual technique for breaking a problem into its component parts. The starting point is a general statement, and the branches of the tree are formed successively, breaking the general statement down into more specific statements.

subprocess—A group of tasks that together accomplish a significant portion of an overall process.

supplier—Anyone from whom the organization receives goods or services.

symptom—A condition where evidence of a problem is manifested.

systems audit—An evaluation of any activity that can affect final product quality.

Taguchi, Dr. Genichi—Taguchi, an internationally honored Japanese engineer, provides his knowledge and experience in training and assisting clients to use robust design, a commonsense, practical approach to optimizing design and production processes.

task—Specific activity necessary in the function of an organization.

team leader—A person who leads a team through the problem-solving process.

team member—A person trained in identifying, analyzing, and solving chronic system problems and identifying improvement opportunities.

theory—An unproven assertion about the reasons for the existence of defects and symptoms.

TQM (total quality management)—Application of quality principles, tools, and techniques to all organizational endeavors including the satisfaction of internal customers. The focus is on defect and cycle time reduction.

trend—A gradual change in a process or product value away from a relatively constant average or level.

$\bar{u}$—The center (average) line of a u-chart.

u-chart—An attribute control chart used to evaluate the number of defectives per subgroup when *n* (subgroup size) is not constant. Unlike the *c*-chart, the *u*-chart is not based on the Poisson distribution. The centerline of the u-chart is *u*.

variable data—Data resulting from quantitative measurements.

variation—A concept stating that no two like items can be completely the same.

VOCT (voice of the customer table)—Used to translate customer verbatims before they are incorporated into the list of *whats* in the quality function deployment (QFD) house of quality.

VRP (variability reduction process)—First developed by the U.S. Department of Defense in the late 1980s, this process uses quality function deployment (QFD), design of experiments (DOE), and statistical process control (SPC), in sequence, to systematically identify and reduce excessive, controllable variation in design and manufacturing processes.

waste—Anything expended on resources that does not add value to the final product. (See *muda*.)

whats—The customer expectations (input variables) in the quality function deployment (QFD) house of quality (customer demands). Customer verbatims are first translated using the voice of the customer table (VOCT) before becoming the *whats*.

X—Notation for an observed data point (value).

$\overline{X}$—Notation for the average of a sample of observed data points (values).

$\overline{\overline{X}}$—Notation for the average of a collection of averages (multiple values of $\overline{X}$).

x̄-R chart—A variable control chart including $\bar{x}$ to track the process average and *R* to track process variability (called an x-bar and R chart).

Z—Notation for the number of standard deviations from the mean (average) to a specific point, for example, Z = 1.96 standard deviations from the mean.

μ—Greek letter *mu*. Notation for the average (mean) value of a population composed of variable (continuous) data points.

ρ—Greek letter *rho*. Notation for the correlation coefficient for a *population*. A number between –1 and +1 that indicates the degree of linear relationship between two sets of numbers.

σ—Greek letter lower case *sigma*. Notation for the standard deviation of a population.

Σ—Greek letter upper case *sigma*. Notation for *the sum of*. All values to the right of Σ should be added together.

Index